## Praise for *Lost to the World*

"Taseer's story alone makes the book a page-turner. A rare story of actual survival from brutal terrorists."

—*Kirkus Reviews*

"What a book. *Lost to the World* is a survival narrative unlike any other. In this unforgettable page-turner, true-life miracles and high-tech death fall from the sky. Our hero endures medieval torments, witnesses acts of sudden kindness, and escapes one surreal prison and battlefield after another. Above all, Shahbaz Taseer's account of his captivity and liberation is, like *Papillon* and *Unbroken*, a deeply moving testament to the triumph of the human spirit."

—Héctor Tobar, Pulitzer Prize–winning author of *Our Migrant Souls*

"Shahbaz Taseer draws you into his endless imprisonment. I was afraid of turning the page, afraid of what lay ahead. I found myself oscillating between tears and laughter. This memoir is a complete tour de force of emotions. I am convinced that it was Taseer's compassion and resilience that kept him alive and that he was guided by the faith he had in his family and the courage instilled in him by his father."

—Sharmeen Obaid-Chinoy, Academy Award–winning filmmaker and journalist

## Shahbaz Taseer

### *Lost to the World*

Shahbaz Taseer is a Pakistani businessman and the son of the late governor of Punjab, Pakistan. Taseer was held in captivity for almost five years and was recovered from Kuchlak, Balochistan, on March 8, 2016. His kidnapping was referred to by *The Guardian* as one of the highest-profile kidnappings in Pakistan.

# Lost to the World

# Shahbaz Taseer

MCD PICADOR FARRAR, STRAUS AND GIROUX NEW YORK

# Lost to the World

A Memoir of
Faith, Family,
and Five Years
in Terrorist
Captivity

MCD
Picador
120 Broadway, New York 10271

Originally published in 2022 by MCD / Farrar, Straus and Giroux
First paperback edition, 2023

Title-page image by Liubou Yasiukovich / Shutterstock.com.

The Library of Congress has cataloged the MCD hardcover edition as follows:
Names: Taseer, Shahbaz, 1983– author.
Title: Lost to the world : a memoir of faith, family, and five years in terrorist
    captivity / Shahbaz Taseer.
Description: First edition. | New York : Farrar, Straus and Giroux, [2022]
Identifiers: LCCN 2022023666 | ISBN 9780374192228 (hardcover)
Subjects: LCSH: Taseer, Shahbaz, 1983– —Kidnapping. | Kidnapping
    victims—Pakistan—Biography. | Victims of terrorism—Pakistan—
    Biography. | Kidnapping—Pakistan—Case studies.
Classification: LCC HV6604.P182 T37 2022 | DDC 362.88/4092 [B]—
    dc23/eng/20220716
LC record available at https://lccn.loc.gov/2022023666

Paperback ISBN: 978-1-250-87223-4

Designed by Abby Kagan

Our books may be purchased in bulk for promotional, educational, or business
use. Please contact your local bookseller or the Macmillan Corporate and
Premium Sales Department at 1-800-221-7945, extension 5442, or by email at
MacmillanSpecialMarkets@macmillan.com.

Picador® is a U.S. registered trademark and is used by Macmillan Publishing
Group, LLC, under license from Pan Books Limited.

For book club information, please email marketing@picadorusa.com.

mcdbooks.com • Follow us on Twitter, Facebook, and Instagram at @mcdbooks
picadorusa.com • Instagram: @picador • Twitter and Facebook: @picadorusa

P1

I am not made from a wood
that burns easily.

# Lost to the World

# 1

**T**he first thing that struck me was the smell.

    I found myself alone in a mud-walled room with straw and animal feces scattered across the dirt floor. My hands and feet were bound with metal cuffs. It was dark; what little light there was slipped in through a small hole in the ceiling where a pipe passed. The stifling heat left me feeling faint. Randomly placed in the corner was a red bucket, which was to serve as my toilet. There was no mattress. The floor would be my bed.

    The pungent odor was the first thing that hit me as I regained consciousness. It was unbearable and turned my stomach. It wasn't just the room that smelled; I did too.

    My immediate thoughts: *Where am I? Will I ever see my family again?*

    Just a few days earlier, I had been at home, in Lahore, Pakistan. It was a normal day like any other. My routine was to wake up, get dressed, and take a ten-minute drive to my workplace. To my complete shock and horror, I was ambushed on my way to work, beaten, and drugged. Waking up to unfamiliar surroundings. Shackled.

This was now my world.

How can your whole life change in an instant? How can everything you know and trust and depend on, every person you love, every comfort you've come to enjoy and embrace, disappear in a moment and be replaced by pain, loneliness, and despair? When that happens, how does one go on?

Would I survive?

These were questions that, it turned out, I would have four and a half years to contemplate.

**As I sat, clueless and groggy, on my very first day in that** sweltering, filthy room, I had more pressing considerations. My natural survival instincts were triggered and I began to make a mental checklist.

Figuring out who had taken me, and why, and what they wanted, and whether I could give it to them and get home safely. As I struggled to get my bearings, two immediate thoughts crossed my mind.

*I must be in Afghanistan. And I'm going to be beheaded.*

I was familiar with stories about kidnappings in Pakistan and knew of people who'd been abducted. In most cases their captors would demand a ransom; however, on occasion it was just to make a gruesome, violent statement, leaving a brutal video for the world as proof of their seriousness and their insanity.

As I'd learn much later, my captors had done both.

I discovered that, less than an hour prior to my arrival, the room I was being held in had been used as a holding pen for sheep to be sacrificed for a Ramzan feast. This, in part, explained the smell. In the punishing late-summer heat, the room stank like a barnyard, or a slaughterhouse. And I didn't smell any better.

It had taken my captors three days to transport me here—wherever "here" was. I assumed I had been ferried to Afghanistan, but it could have been Pakistan. It was hot and dirty, buzzing with mosquitoes. Beyond that, I knew nothing. Clearly, my location didn't matter; I wasn't leaving anytime soon. I was restrained by chains, completely immobilized, similar to a death row criminal. I'd been stripped and dressed in a woman's soiled *shalwar kameez*, now also covered in caked blood and vomit, which I assumed were my own. My jaw was swollen and throbbing, and I had an open wound over one eye. The chains that bound me were fastened to a metal loop in the floor, the kind you'd use to restrain an animal—for example, a sheep—waiting to be killed.

The three days I'd spent traveling to this place were lost to me in a fog. After I was snatched from my car on a busy street in an upscale neighborhood, I'd been blindfolded, beaten, and injected with ketamine, a horse tranquilizer, to keep me unconscious. My captors stuffed me into the back of a car, wedged down on the floor, and kept me out of sight. Whenever I stirred, I was kicked into silence.

On the first day they took me, we eventually arrived . . . somewhere. Having been abducted on a Friday morning, dragged into an empty house blindfolded, I woke up on what I assumed was the following day. One of the captors recklessly pulled the pin from a grenade and placed it in the palm of my hand. He moved within an inch of my face and hissed in my ear in Urdu, "Have you ever held one of these before?" Later, he shoved a gun into my mouth and psychotically asked, "Have you ever seen one before?" I wasn't sure what he wanted me to say. I babbled something about money, about obedience. About how I'd give them what they wanted if they released me.

"You're a valuable treasure," he shouted. "The whole country is looking for you." He yelled so as to frighten me. It definitely worked.

When this man wasn't terrorizing me, he'd reassure me in calming whispers, which was even more unnerving. "Don't worry. You'll be home soon." He explained that he would collect the ransom and release me, and this would all be wrapped up in a day. Maybe two.

His mocking laughter was followed by blows to my head, and a syringe full of ketamine.

Everything about the days right after my kidnapping was obscured in that ketamine haze—a half-remembered barrage of beatings and druggings and barked commands and darkness and barely recollected images. I recall waking up in the back of a car, begging them to stop so I could step outside and urinate. Someone in the car handed me a bottle. They all wore masks. I felt like a ghost, traveling to hell. I started pleading with them to let me step outside by the road to relieve myself. "You've beaten me, you've cuffed me, you've kept me on the floor," I yelled. I kept jabbering. I was petrified.

"I don't need this!" the driver shouted finally. "Put him out!"

More ketamine.

**My next lucid moments were at an army check post on the** outskirts of Lahore. I could barely see. I was in a burka. My captors had disguised me as a woman and sat me up between two of the men in the backseat. As one of the men held a knife to my side, its point perilously close to cutting into me, he whispered, "If I hear a sound, I'll gut you!"

I was unaware that the whole country was looking for me; my kidnapping had become national news. The ISI, Pakistan's intelligence agency, had found the safe house where I'd been held the day before. They'd found my broken sunglasses, and a syringe, used to inject me with ketamine, with samples of my blood in it.

I tried to get a sense of what was happening through the netting of the burka's eyeholes, but the headpiece had twisted to the side. I was drenched from head to toe in perspiration from the searing heat and the ketamine coursing through my body. The heavy black material of the burka clung to me, as stifling as a death shroud. When I'd first regained consciousness, I thought I was in a grave. In a way, I was.

Two young officers, their machine guns slung over their shoulders, gave the car a quick once-over, glancing at all of us, then waved us through.

**Repeatedly injected with ketamine to sedate me, I still had** no idea where we were as we drove into a small town. It was approaching dusk on this early evening, still daytime. My captors drove aimlessly, killing time, waiting until sundown when everyone would break their fast, allowing my captors to spirit me away in the darkness without drawing attention.

As the sun set, the nondescript car was parked. I was moved inside a low, mud-walled building and into the squalid cell where I regained consciousness. This room with the single red bucket and the disgusting, nauseating smell was now my world.

———

**The ketamine forced an uncontrollable vomiting, which** covered me in bile that hardened. I'd never before smelled this putrid in all my life.

My entire body ached from the physical violence from the past few days. Medical attention was certainly not an option.

My captors came and went, wearing scarves to mask their faces. They were young men, I could see that now. One of them looked no older than thirteen. They spoke an unfamiliar language. Later I would learn they were from Uzbekistan. We couldn't communicate or understand one another. The two or three guards in charge ignored me. Alone, I listened to the monstrous buzz of the mosquitoes. They came in great swarms, in and out of that single hole in the ceiling. A deafening racket that still irks me to this day.

I began thinking about *The Matrix*. It was one of my favorite movies. I was obsessed with it when I'd watched it as a teenager. My friends and I ditched our baggy, hip-hop-inspired styles for slim black jeans and slick black overcoats. I got new sunglasses. I saw myself as Neo. I wanted to take a pill and escape the comfortable fantasy world I'd been living in to see how the world really worked, in all its horror and grittiness.

Now it had happened, except someone else had forced the pill down my throat. My old world had disappeared, almost as if it never existed. As though it were a dream, I was in this new world, which felt like a nightmare I couldn't wake up from.

As I sat there, terrified, alone, I wondered if there was any chance of my going back again.

Beyond that, I knew nothing, not where I was, who had taken me, what they wanted, what my family knew, when it would end, or how.

What was undeniable was that I was on my own.

For the very first time in my life, I was completely isolated. Alone.

**If I had known, on that very first day, that I would spend the** next four and a half years of my life in captivity, I do not think I would have made it. The one consolation of my first few days was that I believed that my ordeal would soon be over. My family would find a way to meet my kidnappers' demands and set me free, or they would kill me. It seemed this couldn't drag on for weeks, months, let alone years.

Looking back, I find it hard to believe that's what actually happened.

Yet it did. I know. I was there. I lived through every ugly moment of it.

On the first day, every so often, someone would come in to check on me or drop off a meager meal. Sometimes, they would tell me *he* was coming. *He* was on his way.

"Who?" I would ask.

I had no clue who they were talking about—this man who would hold my life in his hands for the next four and a half years.

Then, one day, weeks later, he arrived.

That's when my ordeal truly began.

# 2

As I write this, I am thirty-five years old, but it's hard to calculate my actual age. Do I include the years wasted in captivity, separated from my family, my friends, and the life I'd built for myself? For ten years, I was married; for more than half that time I was alone. For the five years we were separated, I struggled in darkness, trying to remember my wife's face or recall the sound of her voice. Which anniversary should we celebrate?

For four and a half years I did not hear my name spoken aloud. I was given an alias, Ahmed, or Jee Bhai, which was provocatively meant as a taunt. In Urdu, *jee bhai* is a respectful response, much like saying, "Yes, brother." In the initial days of my captivity, my answer to nearly everything was *Jee bhai*, which led the guards to call me that to berate me. Later, when I found myself in a Taliban prison in a case of mistaken identity, I adopted a new alias, Yusuf Britannia. I reinvented myself as an act of self-preservation. For years, I'd longed to hear my name aloud, but in that prison, I knew if anyone discovered who I really was, it could ring a death knell. My name is Shahbaz Taseer. There is nothing special about me. But I do have a story to tell.

It took not one but many miracles for me to be here to tell it.

## What would you like to know about me?

Did I have a happy childhood? I did, though I now realize it was spent in a bubble of privilege, protecting me from the harsh realities of the world.

My most precious indulgence is waking up to be with my three-year-old daughter. I assure you, I am not particularly brave. I am not particularly strong. I am definitely not a hero, though I do have a better understanding now of what being stoic means.

This is not a story of some amazing qualities I possess. It's the story of what my time in captivity taught me, and how it tested me. I saw the gravest evil, and gestures of kindness too. During that time I was exposed to vile strains of hatred I could never have envisaged. It also inspired me to believe in the power of enduring love. It opened my eyes to the grace that comes when you realize some values are never worth compromising. It made me recognize the ability of the human spirit to endure the unimaginable.

My story is not of what I set out to do; it's simply one of survival and hope, in harsh, hostile, and unfamiliar surroundings.

My parents, Aamna and Salmaan, did everything to secure a warm and loving environment for us to grow up in.

Our home centered around family life and was an open

house where friends knew they were welcome. Our home was warmed by books, art, and sculptures collected over years of travel.

The focal point of the day was outdoor sports. Depending on the weather, it was badminton, table tennis, soccer, or our family favorite, swimming. My father, naturally competitive, was the first to take me and my siblings on and relentlessly beat us for years.

My two younger siblings, Shehryar and Shehrbano, played a pivotal role in my life growing up. To say we were close-knit would be a gross understatement. Being less than two years apart, my brother Shehryar and I share a strong bond with similar interests in sports and music, with plenty of mutual friends. I was always more protective of Shehrbano, who is beautiful, smart, and brave. I have always adored her and tried to be a reliable and supportive big brother. I met Maheen in college, and after a five-year courtship, we were married. It was an exciting new chapter.

**I have many memories of growing up with my father, but** perhaps the most pleasant one was joining my abba in his favorite sun-splashed library, sipping our morning tea, him reading newspapers spread out before him with the TV on broadcasting the latest news updates. He was a morning person, starting his day at 6:00 a.m.

I am the eldest of my parents' three children. Mine was a home bustling with people, full of positive energy.

My father created a media empire with newspapers, magazines, and television channels, founding the largest nationwide cable network. It was important for him to keep up with daily developments. But more than that, he was passionately engaged with the world and wanted us children to be too. He had a library full of books, from floor to ceiling, from Socrates to Jeffrey Archer, and he was always proud to say he'd read every single one of them. There was no activity he enjoyed more than reading, from biographies to books on finance and history to trashy thrillers. "You need to be well-informed!" he'd constantly tell us, which always felt like part encouragement, part scolding. He pushed us to pay as close attention to current events as he did. No one else could be as well-read as my father, but my interests lay elsewhere.

I attended an all-boys institution called Aitchison College, one of the most exclusive private schools in Pakistan. Not very academic, I did just enough work to get by. I was more inclined toward theater, arts, and my passion, music. My younger brother, Shehryar, was the talented athlete of the family, excelling at any sport he chose. The more physically challenging it was, the more competitive he got.

After four years at Aitchison College, I switched schools and enrolled at the Lahore American School (LAS).

In stark contrast to Aitchison College, which was steeped in traditions and the culture of the subcontinent, LAS was an international coeducational school, with a more relaxed environment and a different approach to academics.

I adjusted to the new system, enjoying music, theater, arts, sports, and notably the company of girls in high school. I became popular and made many friends, whom I still remain close to, two decades later.

**My father loved to quote that we are tempered like steel:** "Often we pass through a situation and come out stronger."

He wasn't idly speculating about hardship. I knew all too

well what he had been through. He'd been imprisoned multiple times, including extended bouts of solitary confinement, as punishment for his public protests against Pakistan's military dictator General Zia in the early eighties. My father had been politically active and extremely opinionated, which in Pakistan is a combination that's likely to get you into trouble. As a young man, he had become an admirer of the legendary Zulfikar Ali Bhutto, the president and prime minister of Pakistan in the early 1970s.

My parents were newly married when my father was incarcerated for four months in solitary confinement in Lahore's infamous Fort. Being kept in complete isolation meant no contact with the outside world. It took my young mother many weeks to locate where he was. My father arranged to have a note smuggled out to her by a guard. The letter contained an assurance that has since become part of our family lore: "I am not made of a wood that burns easily." I've often thought of this sentiment ever since.

**That was how my father existed for me in those days:** an inspiring example of being a trailblazer full of courage, clearly a man with focus and a vision. I often wondered if I could ever live up to his legacy.

As a kid growing up under the safety and comfort of his umbrella, I listened to Guns N' Roses and dreamed about college in America. Why would I be worried about solitary confinement or smuggling out assurances to loved ones? My carefree teenage life didn't provide the skill set to cope with a brutal kidnapping.

In hindsight, I realize I'd been living in a bubble. The bubble only became clear to me long after it had burst.

# 3

I n 1961, following an emotional farewell at the Lahore railway station, my father set sail with a one-way ticket via Karachi on a ship that docked at Southampton. This would mark his independent journey toward success. Abba often repeated my grandmother's words to him that day—"Hard work and perseverance are key ingredients to success, my son"—knowing in the back of her mind that a one-way ticket meant he was now on his own and had to carve out his destiny at the age of seventeen. It was a challenging ask, because in the event of failure they would probably never see each other again.

In 1947, post partition, Pakistan was carved out of the Indian subcontinent and my grandfather found himself among the planners and thinkers of the two-nation theory. He was subsequently invited to head one of Pakistan's most prestigious institutes, Islamia College. The historic city of Lahore was to play host, and my British grandmother found herself integrating into the local landscape very comfortably. Making the adjustment even easier was that her sister, Alice, was married to Faiz Ahmed Faiz, who was also a dear friend of my grandfather. The city was old, the country was new, and my grandfather had lived to see his dream of Pakistan come alive. But sadly he died not long after, of a heart attack in 1950, at age forty-seven. His beloved country was three years old. His son, Salmaan, was only six.

Christable, my grandmother, a young widow in a foreign land, made the conscious decision to raise three children as Pakistani Muslims and vowed to keep her late husband's ideals and dreams alive through them. Lahore remained home, and my grandmother's sacrifices amid her determined struggle to do right by her children remained indomitable. She ensured that her children received a good education, which was of paramount importance. Abba attended Saint Anthony's College, a school run by Christian missionaries that laid a solid foundation for his quest to earn his chartered accountancy accreditation.

On returning to Pakistan from England he joined A.F. Ferguson and six months later, bored with being employed, he set himself a challenge to take on some of the largest chartered accountancy firms by establishing one of his own. A forward thinker with a penchant for risk, his success crowded the room. What followed was forays into financial services, telecom, real estate, construction, and media, ultimately earning him the reputation of having the Midas touch.

He became legendary for his business acumen, but his underlying passion and core interest lay in Pakistani politics, in paving the path for democracy to thrive. He joined the Pakistan Peoples Party when it was founded as he was an ardent supporter of its chairman and founder, Zulfikar Ali Bhutto, who was hanged by the ruthless military dictator Muhammad

Zia-ul-Haq. My father authored the first political biography of Mr. Bhutto and took on the power-hungry Zia-ul-Haq. My abba's uncompromising position resulted in years of jail in solitary confinement and torture at the hands of an illegitimate regime, an embarrassing era mostly excluded from Pakistan's history books. In 1988, the usurper Zia-ul-Haq, who had outlived his usefulness, conveniently died, ending more than a decade of martial law. An interim government was formed, which gave Bhutto's stoic and fearless daughter Benazir three months to organize her decommissioned party. My father, who'd worked tirelessly for the restoration of democracy, was awarded a ticket by the Pakistan Peoples Party to contest for a seat in the provincial assembly. His party victoriously swept the election with a two-thirds majority. My father's hard work reaped rewards, resulting in him achieving the highest vote in the election for the Punjab assembly.

This newly established democracy didn't come without its problems, however, with the two most popular parties playing musical chairs for the next decade, during which time Abba opted to reestablish himself in business after failing in his bid for reelection.

In 2008, at the top of his game, he was invited by the federal government to take the oath and govern the province of Punjab. To him this was a great honor and possibly the ultimate form of recognition. Among my father's stellar qualities, the one that stands out with great prominence was his compassion for the underprivileged. One of his first official acts was to pay a visit to Mukhtara Mai, a victim of gang rape who had not received justice. He lent her unconditional support, pledging a grant to her school and vocational center. A few years later the criminal injustice of Asia Bibi's story caught his attention.

Asia Bibi was a poor Pakistani Christian woman who had been sentenced to death over a petty dispute with a group of female villagers over water. The Muslim village women refused to drink from the same well of water as Bibi, claiming she had made it impure. A heated argument ensued, resulting in the women falsely accusing her of insulting the Prophet, a crime punishable by death under the country's draconian blasphemy law authored by the cruel and infamous dictator Zia-ul-Haq. Asia Bibi was arrested, and after a one-sided trial, she was sentenced to death by hanging, a verdict that drew ire and disbelief from around the world. Pope Benedict XVI would later plead for her release.

In the course of a TV interview in 2010, my father was asked his thoughts about the case. He did not mince words. He believed all laws should be discussed in parliament and referred to the blasphemy law as a "black law," which enraged the fanatic right. In November 2010, he held a televised press conference while visiting Asia Bibi in prison, lobbying for clemency, believing strongly that if Pakistan wanted to progress, it had to protect its minorities by revisiting this law.

His comments angered the mullahs, who publicly cried out and placed fatwas on his head demanding his death. Jackals and opportunists in the media leaped on the story, cynically inflaming the controversy, as though his life weren't at risk. My father worked his entire life, in business and in politics, to better his home country, and now religious zealots and self-appointed custodians of the faith turned on him. Abba never stood down when his principles were at stake. Dark forces were assembling to work against him, but he would prevail. He always had.

I couldn't imagine a world without him. But then, I would

soon learn just how much there was that I had yet to understand.

To give context to my story, I had yet to understand the complexities of this region. In 1979, at the height of the Cold War, the U.S.S.R. invaded Afghanistan, prompting the United States to lend support to a very battered Afghan nation. The United States teamed up with Pakistan to develop a mujahideen resistance force of "freedom fighters," who, coupled with local knowledge, Pakistani intelligence and training, and U.S. military hardware, sent the Soviets home in 1989. What was a glorious triumph for the allied world against Red Russia turned out to be a hollow victory for the Afghans. Ten years of war had savaged and completely broken down any system of governance, leading to a state of anarchy in which warlords were the rulers of their domains.

A lawless Afghanistan posed an existential threat to Pakistan, which soon recognized this and set the wheels in motion to protect itself on its porous western border, already home to more than a million displaced Afghan refugees. In the mid-1990s, the warlords, along with some Pakhtun religious clerics and former allies from the war with the Soviet Union, collaborated and formed a group called the Taliban and elected Mullah Muhammad Omar as its head. "Amir ul mominneen," leader of the Muslim *ummah*—"body of people"— was the title given to him, and using that title he formed a *shura* or council to oversee a chain of command that had a structured succession plan along with authority passed on with immediate effect, thus creating a heinous and deadly network never witnessed before. The Taliban was so unique and ferocious that it left Pakistan and the most powerful nations bewildered. Around the world, young, highly impressionable Islamic fundamentalists seduced by this ideology traveled great distances to Afghanistan's most remote and abandoned parts to sign up and dedicate their lives to this cause.

One such man was Muhammad Tahir Farouk, who would become the founding father of the Islamic Movement of Uzbekistan, or IMU. He along with Osama bin Laden conspired to send Abu Musab al-Zarqawi to a previously secular Iraq to sow the seeds of an Islamic jihad. The impact of his efforts brought anarchy and mayhem to Iraq and the region. A reflection of his carnage is what we see today in Iraq and Syria, in the institution informally known as the Islamic State. This powerful trio of bin Laden, Omar, and Farouk proudly bear responsibility for terrorist organizations from North Africa across the Middle East and into South Asia.

I found myself in this minefield of terror and intrigue, a prisoner, helpless and unable to make sense of how my family would fulfill the requirements of these mercenaries.

# 4

I n 2001, I was seventeen, a senior in high school in Lahore, dreaming of attending university in the United States. A number of my close friends were American. We holidayed abroad every summer.

My family was fortunate enough to have traveled the world, mostly to Europe and the Far East, including a memorable safari in Kenya. While it's hard to imagine any place being more alive than Lahore, at the time a raucous city of 6 million people that was constantly in motion, the draw of a future in America was exciting and appealing. It was definitely where I felt I belonged.

Then 9/11 happened.

This great tragedy occurred a world away from me. As a teenager, watching these events unfold in another country, on another continent, I couldn't comprehend that this heinous act would have any direct impact on me. It was dark and sinister, but it had nothing to do with me. It appeared that the nineteen terrorists, unstable and brainwashed, were all

Muslim. America and its music culture and the American dream was where my interests were focused.

At seventeen, I was young, fearless, and politically naive, but the events of that day impacted both my personal life and the socioeconomic lives of my countrymen. Many foreign families were resettled without notice, as Lahore was deemed unsafe for them.

How had our country suddenly become so dangerous overnight that people were fleeing?

For Pakistan, 9/11 changed everything. It led to the American war in Afghanistan, which sadly continued, with no clear objectives. A common feature of this aggression was drone strikes, which caused thousands of civilian casualties in both Afghanistan and Pakistan, as collateral damage. I say this as someone who is both in favor of drone strikes and a survivor of two of them.

Inevitably, the fighting and chaos in Afghanistan spilled over into Pakistan, across a porous border that was illegally breached by violent militias carrying dangerous weapons, and virulent anger. In Pakistan, 9/11 led to a chilling rise in deadly terrorist attacks, driven by extremists angered that our country had allied itself with the United States. Lahore, the vibrant city of my youth, full of streetlights and colorful flower boxes, along with every other large city in Pakistan, quickly became an intimidating fortress of high walls, barbed wire, and army checkpoints. Suicide bombings at mosques, or crowded markets, became a numbingly common occurrence. Soon, it no longer made sense to talk about any place in Pakistan as a "tourist destination" as this industry had dried up completely. Mention Pakistan now to the average American and they're most likely to think of rubble and chaos with a travel advisory, which is not the country I grew up in or the one I live in now.

The ascendant religious extremism that led to 9/11 also affected my family in personal and painful ways. The attacks on 9/11 unleashed a dangerous new fervor that eventually, over a decade later, resulted in my father's assassination. The DNA of my kidnapping harks back to this rise in bigotry.

My family, like many others, paid the highest possible price, unquestionably a direct consequence of what happened in New York City on that day. It was unthinkable that as a naive teenager, watching the news in a city far away from where the terrorist attacks took place, I could have imagined any of the events that unfolded following this.

I know I'm not alone in how that day affected me. Many lives were lost, shattered, and irrevocably changed. But that an event so distant could crumble my world was a rude awakening for my young self. It was the first time that my bubble of privilege and protection started to wobble and threatened to burst.

**Now a huge portion of the world was cut off to me. So, my** family decided, I would go to school in London.

My father was the ultimate raconteur, embellishing stories of his travels as a young man, further igniting my desire to seek out accumulated wisdom and discover the riches of the West.

I graduated from school and enrolled at SOAS University of London to begin my foundation year in international law. These were exciting times for me as this would be my first taste of life away from the comfort and security of my parents' home. Looking into the rearview mirror as I left Lahore eager to take on new challenges and opportunities, I was full of optimism and hope, as the world was my oyster.

But my early days in London were in stark contrast to my

expectations, as I only realized then how much the world had changed since 9/11. This was not the United Kingdom offering the opportunities my father and grandfather had enjoyed as students. I was made uncomfortably aware of my skin, my religion, my culture, and my race in a whole new and unwelcome way. In all my years growing up in Lahore, I had never been subject to any form of prejudice or racism.

For the first time in my life, the word "Muslim" was spoken, in many countries, including the United Kingdom, with equal parts hatred, suspicion, and fear. It was widely said all Muslims are not terrorists, but all terrorists are Muslim. I spent many summers growing up holidaying in London. Despite the fact that both my maternal and paternal grandmothers were British, this was the first time I was made to feel like an unwelcome outsider.

Pakistan is the fifth most populous country in the world, with a population of 220 million, ranking just after China, India, the United States, and Indonesia. Pakistan's customs and culture vary as much as the sandy coastline of Sindh and the deserts of Balochistan differ from the lush plains of Punjab and the jagged snowcapped peaks of the north, some of which are among the highest mountains in the world. Pakistan is a country of multiple ethnicities, but one ideal: people should coexist in harmony.

As with most countries, Pakistan is no exception in not having lived up to that ideal. Patriots such as my father lent their voices to the plight of minorities.

**In 2010, about a year before I was kidnapped, I took my** wife on a long-planned trip to California. Overall, it was a wonderful, if slightly exhausting, trip.

The journey from California to Lahore is an especially long haul, almost twenty-four grueling hours in total flight time. We arrived at SFO airport and boarded our plane to New York. The flight was delayed and delayed further. We sat with our fellow passengers, restless and waiting for updates. I tried to settle in and catch some sleep.

FBI agents boarded the aircraft, arrested the two of us, and took us off the plane.

It's hard to express just how humiliating it is to be led in handcuffs off a plane full of strangers, all of whom assume you are criminals, terrorists, or worse. I'll always be grateful for one sympathetic young college kid who stood up and started making a video on his smartphone and telling the officers this was an injustice, that we were being racially profiled. He was right. There was no other explanation for it.

They pushed my wife and me into separate cars. I could see Maheen sitting in the back seat of her car, looking confused, outraged, and worried. I tried to mouth some words to her to reassure her, so she wouldn't feel anxious. But the agents saw us trying to communicate, so they repositioned the cars so we could no longer see each other.

Meanwhile, the remaining passengers were being evacuated. The FBI agent informed us that someone had made an anonymous call about the flight, claiming a bomb threat. By now, a bomb disposal unit had arrived on the tarmac and was boarding the plane with dogs to search the cabin. As far as Maheen and I knew, there might well have been a bomb on board, a terrifying prospect. We also knew for sure that we weren't responsible for it. Watching all this unfold, both Maheen and I had the same thoughts, in our separate vehicles. *Apparently, everyone thinks we were going to blow up this plane. And now they have left us here, parked under the wing, while they search for a bomb. If there is a bomb on board, and it goes off, we'll not only explode along with the plane, but we'll forever be blamed for being the ones who planted it. They'd say, "We got the right people. They were guilty all along."*

Maheen and I sat on the tarmac for another hour or so, before the agents finally drove us to the terminal. Again, we were kept separate—I was led to one room while my wife was taken to another; we weren't given a chance to speak. After sitting in the plane for hours, then on the tarmac, I was beyond embarrassed—I was outraged.

When I reached the small interrogation room, two agents greeted me and pulled the good-cop / bad-cop routine on me. It was like a scene out of *Lethal Weapon*. The bad cop barked, "Do you know why you're here?"

"Not really. But I did see a bomb disposal unit."

"You're here because we suspect you tried to hijack and bomb that plane. And we're checking your bags right now for bombs and ammunition."

"The only thing inside my bag that's even slightly suspicious is an iPad that I just bought. And it's still in the plastic wrap. So, if you open it and find a bomb inside, that's Apple's fault, not mine."

I answered all of their questions honestly and forthrightly, but I didn't react with anything like calm or poise. My anger at being singled out like this—at being hauled from our flight in handcuffs because someone thought a Pakistani man in a Lakers jersey and his wife wearing a beanie must obviously be a couple of terrorists—spilled over. Ever since 9/11, if you fly internationally on a Pakistani passport, you can expect undue attention. You will be pulled "randomly" from lines for extra security screening and be subjected to rigorous questioning by anyone whose job is guarding a border. Still, I'd always thought of myself as westernized, I fit right in. I was Shabby T! I went to an American school. I listened to American music. I could recite whole Jay-Z albums from memory. My favorite junk food is McDonald's. There's nothing quite like twenty pieces of McNuggets.

None of this mattered to the agents questioning me or to the people who'd profiled us and made that call. To them, I was a Pakistani, and that meant a terrorist. We'd come for a relaxing vacation and now we were each stuck in a windowless room, defending ourselves against charges of terrorism.

At one point, frustrated, I may have pulled the "Do you know who I am?" card.

They did not know.

"My father is Salmaan Taseer. He's the serving governor of Punjab province. Right now, Senator John Kerry is with my father distributing flood relief aid in Pakistan. Hillary Clinton has been to the governor's house for tea."

Lest I forget to mention, being the governor's son, I was entitled to an official passport, known as the blue passport.

Slowly, I could see it dawn on both the good cop and the bad cop that they'd gotten it horribly wrong. It's one thing to pull a random person off a commercial aircraft and label him a terrorist. It's another when that person's father is a high-serving official known to the U.S. secretary of state.

Their whole tone changed. They began damage control.

They apologized for the mix-up. My wife and I were reunited; she was equally traumatized.

To compensate for their behavior, the agents picked up our suitcases and led us through an empty luggage hall toward the exit doors. On one level, I understood they were simply doing their jobs, protecting innocent people from real threats. I also accepted that this was a new reality. It evoked mixed feelings of not only anger and resentment but also sadness that the world, as we knew it, had descended into such a dark place where racial profiling had been legalized.

As we were leaving, an agent stopped us and said, "By the way, you guys might get these media people coming at you. Just ignore them. Let that go. Just go home safely!"

My friend Harris and his father met us outside the terminal. Harris's dad was sympathetic, comforting us as he helped us into the car. Harris, meanwhile, was insisting that he knew a good lawyer if we wanted to sue.

Then my phone rang.

It was my father calling, deeply concerned. "I just heard the news, are you okay?"

I was rattled and much shaken, but I didn't convey that to my father, who always said I was the most stoic person he knew.

Despite all this, my bubble of privilege was more or less intact. I had my family, my home, my work, my life. I thought nothing could shake those fundamental truths.

I was wrong about that too. Even before I was kidnapped, life had one more unfortunate awakening for me.

# 5

**W**riting about the fourth of January has possibly been the most difficult chapter of this book. The pain and loss of that day makes everything else pale by comparison. The fourth of January 2011 should have been a day of celebration as it was the twenty-fifth birthday of my brother, Shehryar. My father and Shehryar had spent a couple of days in Islamabad for work and were scheduled to return for an evening of festivities at home, which had been planned by my mother.

Shehryar called to say he was leaving by road and Abba would conclude his official commitments and fly in in time for the party. I ended the call and walked across to my mother's bedroom, where she was engrossed in an animated conversation with my father, and I asked if I could have a quick word with him.

He sounded cheerful and busy, in a great mood. He was happiest and content when a million challenges lay ahead of him. As we spoke, he was strolling through the quaint but bustling Kohsar Market with his official security detail. "I've had my soup, I've got my book, and I'm a happy camper" he told me.

"I see on the news your government's coalition has broken. Does this mean you will be out of a job?" I replied jokingly.

"Yeah, yeah, I have heard this a million times before. Just remember there will always be the appointed and the disappointed! So join the queue and get in line!" he said with his usual joie de vivre.

As I laughed and soaked up his wit, I had no idea these would be his last words to me.

Our family home is centered around a courtyard. On one side, you can see into my father's library and on the other is my parents' lounge. The courtyard itself was always very special to me. It's where my father's day would start. Every morning at eight I would join him for breakfast and an engaging conversation, our special time together, which I cherished. The conversation always centered around current affairs and our family business.

That day, as I stood outside in the courtyard, excited to be reunited with both my father and brother and eager for the birthday celebration to begin, I heard my phone ringing. It was Tammy, my aunt, or *khala*.

She asked if I was watching the news.

"Why? What happened?"

"There has been an incident, possibly an explosion, in Kohsar Market," she said worriedly.

My mind went in all directions in a panic.

I prayed this was a mere coincidence as moments earlier my father and I had been speaking on the phone.

"Abba is in Kohsar Market," I said.

I'm not sure what she said next. I wasn't listening anymore. I hung up and ran inside the house.

My mind was racing with fear. Terror attacks and explosions were not uncommon in Pakistan. Some part of me deep inside already knew that, if there'd been an incident at the market, it must have involved my father. He was too high-profile and controversial for me to pretend that this was a coincidence.

I'd just been speaking with him. It didn't seem possible that so much could have changed in a flash.

When I entered my mother's room, I found her composed and looking perfectly normal, but on seeing me, she knew something was wrong. "What is it, Beta?" she said—*beta* being a term of endearment for a son. I didn't answer her. I was busy dialing my father's number on my cell phone.

No answer—but his phone was ringing, which I took as a good sign. *Maybe he's been distracted by whatever is happening in the market*, I thought. *Maybe he'll pick up when I call him back.*

I called back.

This time the phone was off.

My mother could see I was panicking and kept pressing me to tell her what was going on.

"Aunt Tammy just called and said there's been an incident in Kohsar Market." I dialed my father's number again.

*Pick up, pick up, pick up. Tell me you are safe. Tell me this is nothing.*

My mother's face went white as a sheet. "What kind of incident?"

His phone was still off. No answer.

I hung up and called his military secretary.

When I got through, he said, "I heard as well. I'm on it." Otherwise, he had no news for us.

A sense of frantic urgency set in, even as we realized we could do nothing but wait. These moments felt like the longest and most desperate of my life. I looked at my mother. I wasn't sure what to tell her. We both stood there in silence.

Then her phone rang. It was Tammy again. "Turn on the TV."

Kohsar Market, in one of Islamabad's affluent neighborhoods, is a vibrant hot spot packed with restaurants and cafés to which diplomats and journalists gravitate.

On TV, the images were chaotic and confusing. Clearly something catastrophic had occurred, but we couldn't tell what. It didn't look as if an explosion had happened, but something bad definitely had.

Then the TV anchorman announced, "We're getting reports that the governor has been shot."

There was no further news, so I immediately put in another call to my father's military secretary. Unable to get through, I left word, asking that he call me right away. By this time, my brother had arrived. No one was thinking about his birthday or the planned celebrations. We were glued to the TV, waiting for news. But none was coming. My mother couldn't take the uncertainty, so she headed out to the garden with my sister and brother to wait.

**A few minutes later, my phone rang. It was Colonel Haider.**

I took his call in the courtyard.

"What is happening?" I was distraught. Clearly, from the news reports, *something* had happened to my father. I wanted the colonel to tell me my father was safe, he was going to be okay, that they were rushing him to hospital, to the attention of the best doctors in the country. I wanted to hear the colonel say my father would soon be home, reunited with us, as he'd promised he would be, just a few minutes earlier.

Instead, the colonel said, "Shahbaz, we're going to bring him back."

"What? Why?" I was confused and angry. This made no sense. My father needed to be in the hospital, I argued. He needed the best care that doctors could provide. He did not need to be flown back to us in Lahore. That sounded incredibly dangerous. No, we would go to see him. We would get on the next flight.

"Listen, you have to understand what I'm saying. We're bringing his body back."

I barely remember what happened after that. I know the phone dropped from my hand. I know I stumbled out of the courtyard and back into the sitting room where my mother and family were waiting.

Friends began filling our home.

I meandered through the small crowd toward my mother, feeling an insane sense of emptiness that is hard to describe, even now. This feeling that your whole world has fallen apart. Barely having processed it myself, I now had to break this news to my mother.

"Mama. Abba's gone."

Despite the trials and tribulations of my four-and-half-year ordeal in captivity, as I look back, this was the singularly most difficult and painful moment of my life. No child should be cursed with this burden.

I never say that my father *died*. I never describe it that way. My maternal grandfather died, at the end of a long and meaningful life. I've known other people who've passed away. But my father didn't *die*. *Die* sounds too passive, too natural. My father was snatched, senselessly murdered in cold blood.

After the news was delivered, everything became chaotic and the hours passed in a manic haze. Life had taken from me the person I admired the most in the world, leaving me alone and shattered without even a chance to say goodbye.

At first, I clung to the crazy notion that maybe he'd survived. Shot, yes, but one or two bullets couldn't bring down the man I knew. He was Salmaan Taseer! A figure larger than life. Then we heard: it was not one bullet, but twenty-seven. These bullets were delivered by his own security guard, Mumtaz Qadri. How was this possible? My father had been cut down in cold blood by a lunatic riled up by the hateful words of clerics. These so-called religious leaders had called for my father's head because he spoke out in defense of Asia Bibi. Now Mumtaz Qadri, one of my father's guards, had quite literally answered their calls. A man entrusted with my father's protection shot him in the back like a puny coward instead. The killer was arrested on the spot. The only mystery was why fate had allowed a man as despicable as that to so casually end the life of a man like my abba.

Later, I'd recall a time walking through Lahore's old city streets with my abba, just the two of us. Concerned for his safety, I asked where his security detail was. Ironically he flippantly replied, "And who will guard the guards?" He said, "To live in constant fear is to not live at all." He wanted to be free to stroll the streets of the city he loved, in the country that was always his home. The same country he believed in unconditionally, fighting for its liberty and freedom. He wanted to feel that freedom. Today all he wanted was some soup and to browse for a book. Now his own guard had betrayed him. My father was a symbol of peace in my country; the example I'd aspired to all my life was no more.

**That evening the body was transported back to Lahore in a** military aircraft with Shehryar and me there to receive him. A huge steel coffin was unloaded and placed on the tarmac. Despite its size it was difficult to comprehend my father could be confined to such a box.

The streets had been cordoned off and traffic blocked to give clear passage to the ambulance from the airport to our home. Normally a ten-minute drive, it seemed an eternity as I sat next to my father apologizing that I was not with him. I hadn't been there to protect him.

We brought him home and placed the coffin in our drawing room, where he was to lie until the official state funeral with a twenty-one-gun salute the following morning. The government declared three days of mourning, awarding him the highest civilian honor, Shaheed-e-Insaniyat, which translates to "martyred for humanity."

Messages of condolences poured in from the whole world, from people in every walk of life. Among them was Hillary Clinton, then U.S. secretary of state, whom I'd met when she'd visited our family home. She strongly condemned the killing of my father and released a statement declaring she "admired his work to promote tolerance and education of Pakistan's future generations. His death is a great loss."

A sea of mourners attended the funeral. Beyond the thousands there to mourn him in person, millions more mourned him remotely. To many, as he was the last living hope for a prosperous, secular, and peaceful Pakistan, his murder spoke of dark times ahead. My father fought for the powerless and embodied the best of the dreams of our country's founder, Muhammad Ali Jinnah.

Although I shared the grief of my countrymen, what my family was experiencing was much more personal.

In the days following my father's death, there were also those who celebrated his killer, Mumtaz Qadri. These zealots celebrated the senseless murder of a man who gave his life protecting the most vulnerable members of our society.

Supporters of Qadri, including members of the legal fraternity, showered the killer with rose petals as he arrived at the court for his hearing. Others kissed his cheeks and endorsed his actions while cheering in support. My father's death had, it was said, exposed how far our country still had to go before tolerance and justice could truly be embraced.

In the aftermath of the assassination, my mother received multiple death threats. An undetonated grenade precariously placed outside her office was discovered, and my sister received photographs of beheaded bodies in the mail telling her she was next. Watching the news made it clear that tens of thousands of right-wing extremists celebrated my father's death and would happily rejoice in my family's as well.

But we weren't going anywhere. My family was approached by the U.S. consul general, inquiring if we needed to relocate to the United States for political asylum. My brother and I declined the offer. My father was no more, but I chose not to live as a secondary citizen in a foreign country.

Very little added up or made sense. Even as I felt an upsurge in supportive love from the people closest to us, for the first time my family and I were truly vulnerable. Our loss and overwhelming sadness were now being overshadowed by another danger. My mother summoned Shehryar and me after a meeting with our family lawyer. He had cautioned her in no uncertain terms about the variables in my father's business affairs. The lawyer pointed out many loose ends that could lead to financial ruin if they were not tied up and addressed immediately. Our business like many others was still recovering from the backlash of the 2008 global recession. Friends had become enemies, bankers had become ruthless debt collectors, and family had become estranged. The vultures were circling overhead and the sharks were swimming between our feet. All were positioning to find profit in our misfortune and move in for the kill.

My mother, who had lived happily as an indulged housewife all her life and had never dealt with commercial matters, saw these opportunists licking their chops. They would come in the dead of night, she told me, and steal business from us. But when she said this, I saw she wasn't panicking or in any way afraid. Instead she was focused and determined. This resolve ultimately served her and to some extent me as well during what lay ahead for both us.

The focus shifted solely to protecting our interests.

In the coming months, through tireless work, we stabilized our affairs. After carefully consolidating our position, we understood that, while still not out of the woods, we could now breathe life back into our business group. Despite a climate of hate and the adverse conditions facing us in our country, we would not be leaving Pakistan anytime soon.

The earth seemed to be settling beneath my feet as I now directed a charged focus on resolving work issues. Shehryar and I had been trained by the best mentor, and now it was time to prove our grit. This was life 2.0; although nothing would be like it was before, I was trying to bring a semblance of order back into my family's lives. Who was to know that on the twenty-sixth of August 2011 as I got into my car to go to my office that my life was about to change in the most violent manner.

# 6

On the morning of August 26, 2011, as usual I woke up before my alarm, which was set for 6:30 a.m. As I was getting dressed for work, my wife, perhaps intuitively, urged me to skip the office. Not being a morning person, she wanted to have breakfast and catch up.

I was having none of it. Eager to share the good news I'd brought back from my travels to Dubai, reassuring her of my undivided attention once the weekend came around, I set out purposefully.

Smart casual is the standard office garb, only this time I sported a newly won trophy: a Bulgari watch I had won in a senseless bet against my dear friend Hassan Elahi a week earlier.

It had been a fun night, and pretty typical of my time spent with my friends, most of whom I've known since childhood. We are a tight-knit group that grew up together, hence they are like family to me. I won't go so far as to say the happiest times of my life were hanging out with my friends, but it's definitely the time when I feel like myself in a room full of familiar faces—that's when Shabby T comes alive.

That particular night felt like a bonus. I had wrapped up my business dealings and managed an earlier flight to go back home. As the plane took off for the three-hour flight from Dubai to Lahore, I settled into my seat with my usual mix of exhaustion and preflight anxiety. I have never been a big fan of flying, so I usually have a few movies downloaded on my iPad to watch as a distraction. I watched *A Mighty Heart*, a movie about Daniel Pearl, the American journalist kidnapped in Karachi, Pakistan, held hostage, and later beheaded by his abductors.

I did not know it was the last movie I would see for nearly five years. Or that soon I would live my own version of it.

**That fateful Friday morning, per my routine, I walked to-**ward my car, where my guard was waiting to accompany me on the short and normally uneventful journey to the office. My car battery had been giving me trouble lately, and as I cranked the engine, the car refused to start.

Parked conveniently nearby was my late father's Mercedes coupe, which I climbed into. The car is a cozy two-seater, affording little room for a bulky guard. Plus, an array of electronic gadgets and a briefcase now took up the second seat. I waved away my guard, instructing him to get my SUV repaired.

After my father's assassination, I developed a natural aversion to traveling with armed guards. On many occasions, I intentionally left the guard at home and was emotionally reprimanded by my worried mother, constantly concerned for her family's safety. To allay her fears and to placate her, I would usually make an exception. Clearly, I had an excuse here. The sports car had no room for the bulky guard, a decision I will regret for a long time to come.

Unceremoniously setting off on the ten-minute drive to my office, I made a mental checklist, preparing myself to update my colleagues.

I had a feeling it was going to be a good day. Sadly, that was not to happen.

**Here's what I didn't know.**

As I left my neighborhood, a spotter named Farhaj Butt was waiting to notify his accomplices that I was on my way. I wasn't in the car they expected, and because the Mercedes is low to the ground, he missed me. The next spotter, Usman Basra, didn't. He was positioned at a crucial point on my route, an intersection where I'd typically choose to go one way or another. My mother had always insisted on the importance of taking different, random routes to work, a precaution against kidnappings and robberies. These dangers and hazards were prevalent in Pakistan; I neglected to pay heed. I was a creature of habit. I took my usual turn.

I crossed the bridge that takes you away from a cantonment residential area into Gulberg, a more commercial hub buzzing with restaurants, offices, and other public spaces, where men like my abductors go undetected. Basra relayed my position by phone. He notified a car full of men that I was on my way and which route I was taking. They set their plan into motion.

A week earlier, this same crew had sent Basra to scale a telephone pole on our block to install a video camera overlooking our home so they could watch my brother and me as we came and went. They wanted to understand our daily routine. We had no idea about any of this. A local street cleaner had passed by and startled Basra, so he never finished installing the camera. Even so, the crew already had a good idea of what time I usually left, where I went, and how best to intercept me. This team had done their homework and were perfectly aware of my movements.

I should also mention that the roads I travel to work aren't hidden, treacherous back alleys. They're busy commercial streets in the middle of an upscale neighborhood in Lahore. The cantonment, as the neighborhood is called, is a housing division controlled by the army. There are security checks at every point of entry and you need valid ID to get in or out. The idea that anything could happen to me in my short drive from home to work simply seemed unthinkable. This was my comfort zone. I remained oblivious of any danger, feeling no need for caution.

**As I drove onto the street just a block from the office,** parked inconspicuously on the side was a car packed with men. Quite naturally, I thought nothing of it. As I passed the car, I noticed one man in particular. He smiled at me. A strange smile. As though we knew each other. I thought he was just admiring my car. I later realized he was smiling because, so far, the crew's plan was going perfectly.

Having passed their vehicle, the man stepped out, and I could clearly see he was holding a gun. He pointed his pistol at me. The other four men jumped out of the car, screaming and waving weapons menacingly, creating chaos and confusion. A few had pistols, and one held an automatic Kalashnikov rifle. They rushed at me, surrounding the car; uncharacteristically, I did not panic. I remained calm. My first thought was *This is a robbery. These things happen in life.* I could see that I was in for a bit of trouble, but I assumed it would be over quickly. I'd hand over my wallet, watch, and electronic devices. That was the norm, or so I thought.

The only valuable I wanted to protect, other than my life, was my car.

*I don't want them to get my car.*

In my defense, it was not my car.

As the gunmen approached my vehicle, shouting at me and brandishing their weapons, I had the presence of mind to drop the car keys into the door panel. If this was a carjacking, at least I could make it more difficult for them.


**In hindsight, I realize the value of a car pales in comparison** to the value of one's life. I should just have let them take the car. I assumed they would take my money and my watch and be gone as quickly as they came. A simple holdup.

But this was not to be. It wasn't a carjacking, either. They made it abundantly clear.

I was the prize.

All of which started to dawn on me when one of the men yanked open my door and violently dragged me from the driver's seat. His accomplice approached me to throw a hood over my head.

The smiling man put a gun to my head and whispered words that remain indelible in my memory:

"I've come for you, Shahbaz."

———

**When I recalled those moments later, I'd have plenty of** time to think about them, hours and days and months to sit alone and scrutinize every detail. I wondered how things might have gone differently. The what-ifs remained unanswered, swirling in my mind. What if I'd taken a different car that morning? What if I'd heeded my wife's advice and stayed home? What if I'd lingered in Dubai for the weekend as my old friend Sikander had urged me to do? What if my guard had traveled to work with me that day? I knew better than to regret that last one, though, that he didn't accompany me. From what I learned about my captors over the next four years, I know they would simply have murdered him.

Once my captors had slipped that hood over my head, I had no more time to think. I heard shouting as they argued over what to do next. They hustled me into the back of their car, a cramped Toyota Corolla. I couldn't tell what was happening, but I heard a lot of screaming. I was probably screaming too, a pure adrenaline reaction. It might even have looked funny if you were standing there watching us. A bunch of grown men shouting and yelling in a panic in the middle of the street, like something from an old slapstick comedy film.

I could tell that my kidnappers were panicking. Their plan was already fraying. They had to get off the street before they drew too much attention. I didn't fully understand this at the time—I had a hood over my head. Plus, I was being physically assaulted. After they shoved me into the backseat we took off, leaving the fifth man behind to follow in my car. Or at least that was their plan.

But there was no key in my car.

With all of us jammed into the car, the kidnappers yelled at me and at each other. They kept punching me to keep me quiet until, finally, one of them drugged me with a syringe of ketamine, a tranquilizer normally used on horses.

I don't remember much of what happened after that.

Many years later, I pieced together how my impulsive act of hiding the car keys in the door panel was the smartest decision I'd made.

**My brother Shehryar got the news in Karachi when he** landed from Lahore. "Shahbaz has been kidnapped." Word of the scuffle in the street had traveled to employees in my office with news that I had been taken. To the first people who heard it, it sounded absurd. Taken? What? Where? *How?* But Shehryar knew immediately something was wrong.

He had the presence of mind to contact the concerned authorities in the intelligence agencies, an important wing of the army.

**When the agents arrived at the scene, my car was still in** the street. They'd already initiated surveillance called geofencing, by which they'd monitor the activity and movement of all cell phones through voice recognition, in the hope of tracing the kidnappers. Sadly, it was not successful, owing to severe traffic congestion of the last working day of the week.

The authorities also moved swiftly to activate a perimeter of roadblocks and checkpoints, in hopes of snaring the kidnappers before they left the city. Lahore is a sprawling metropolis, but there are only so many main roads in and out.

The net was closing in. Surely it would catch them. My ordeal would be over in a matter of hours. Or so my family prayed.

Except that, in the chaotic hour or so after I'd been taken, no one had yet communicated to the checkpoint officers what model of car my captors were driving. They were simply stopping cars and inspecting them briefly.

Other obstacles, other checkpoints, had to be bypassed before you could leave the city. I did not think of myself as a target, but because of my father's stature in the country, the authorities were moving quickly to ensure my return. The assumption was that my captors would attempt to spirit me to one of the lawless areas in the remote outlands of Pakistan, which, in the end, is what they did. This is the usual pattern in high-profile kidnappings. Snatch someone off the streets of a city and move them to a safe house in a remote area hospitable to extremists.

But my captors were smart, at least about this. They didn't try to leave the city at all. Not at first.

# 7

**A**s my abductors sped away from the scene, all hell broke loose. I was drugged, unconscious, hidden in the footwell. The ketamine had knocked me out completely. On the occasional, brief moments when I regained consciousness, I was disoriented and clueless. I was unaware that, for the first thirty-six hours after I was snatched, the security and intelligence agencies and electronic media, along with every echelon of society, were focused on the unfolding of this high-profile incident.

I wouldn't learn about any of this until months or years later. Some I learned from my captors, the rest long after I was freed. For example, I was to find out years later that my impulsive concealing of my car keys had both saved my life and would continue to keep me alive.

As my captors sped away, a man named Abdur Rehman, carrying a Kalashnikov, broke protocol by staying behind, greedily eyeing the Mercedes as a trophy to bag. He was a telecom engineer in his early twenties residing in Lahore, unremarkable looking and mild mannered—certainly not optics that I would associate with a terrorist.

Along with his brother, Noshab Rehman, another of my kidnappers, Abdur had been radicalized while still at engineering university. Both of them played an important role in the first sequence of my abduction.

Deviating from the original plan, Abdur Rehman decided unilaterally to take the sports car and planned to drive it to the safe house where I was to be held. There was one problem: when he got into my car, no keys were to be found.

He panicked and used his cell phone to call one of the spotters in the vicinity. This link led the authorities to their first breakthrough. Minutes after the call, Usman Basra arrived on a motorcycle to pick up Abdur Rehman.

Basra was not just another low-level conspirator. He was a trusted friend and right-hand man to the ringleader of the whole operation. This ringleader was the man who'd smiled at me from the car as I drove by and, I learned later, was the man who'd whispered to me, "I've come for you, Shahbaz." He called himself Muhammad Ali. He was the most evil man I will ever meet.

Usman Basra was not just Muhammad Ali's valued lieutenant; he was also engaged to marry Muhammad Ali's fourteen-year-old sister-in-law. So, Basra was not just an expendable lackey. He was like a brother to Muhammad Ali. This made a huge difference in my case. But only because Basra got caught.

When Basra arrived on his motorcycle, the pickup did not go smoothly. The two men got into a heated argument over whether to bring the weapon. Basra, understandably, felt that it would attract too much attention to be carrying a machine gun as they sped away from the scene of a kidnapping. But

Abdur Rehman apparently didn't want to leave his beloved gun behind. Eventually, Basra prevailed and convinced him to discard the rifle.

Basra, to conceal his identity, was wearing a helmet, with his cell phone precariously placed in it. He hit a ditch in the road and the phone jostled free and dropped into the street. In all the panic and chaos, Basra didn't notice. His focus was to escape the crime scene, and this cheap, disposable phone became pivotal in revealing the identity of the terrorists.

These two events, the breaking of protocol to try to snatch the car, and the use and subsequent loss of the cell phone, were the two big breakthroughs that led to the first piece of the puzzle.

Additionally, as I found out much later, two weeks before I'd been kidnapped, another high-profile abduction had taken place. A U.S. national, Warren Weinstein, was an aid worker/contractor living in Lahore, in an affluent area known as Model Town. Weinstein was cautious and traveled with highly trained ex-commando guards. He'd been grabbed as part of an intricately planned operation staged during Ramzan, when a gang of extremists distracted his guards with the offer of a feast, then stormed his compound and abducted him. I didn't know anything about this. I'd never heard of Weinstein. The story had barely made the news. Plus, I had been traveling. Over the next four years, our fates became strangely intertwined. We would wind up miles apart, in the dangerous, unpoliced mountains of Pakistan. Sadly, only one of us would make it back alive. In the hours and days after my abduction, the investigation into Weinstein's kidnapping led to an improbable, near-miraculous breakthrough in the investigation of my kidnapping.

**The ISI agents arrived at the crime scene within an hour of** my being taken. At first, they had nothing. No clues, no obvious evidence, and no initial theories about who might have abducted me or why. Their geofencing wasn't turning up any useful leads. The assumption was that this was a typical kidnapping for ransom, likely conducted by al-Qaeda-related extremists or by the Tehreek-e-Taliban, as the Pakistani Taliban is known. Both groups had a history of such operations. The ISI agents believed that the modus operandi would be to whisk me out of the city as quickly as possible, then contact my family with ransom demands. If the demands were met, I would be released. If they weren't, I would most definitely be killed. Victims were usually slaughtered as an example to the next targets and their families.

The ISI officer in charge of investigating my abduction was Colonel Kiyani, a veteran investigator with a kind face and a well-trimmed mustache. Kiyani had an excellent reputation due to his tireless work ethic. When he arrived to inspect my crime scene with his deputies, he'd simultaneously been working on the Weinstein case. They'd already identified a few suspects in that abduction. One suspect, an engineering student, told the ISI that he'd been convinced by a friend to acquire a vacant house to be used as a potential safe house. The name of that friend: Usman Basra.

At that point, Basra was only peripherally linked to the Weinstein kidnapping and not yet connected to mine. Kiyani and his team found no evidence to lead to a breakthrough. As the team interrogated eyewitnesses, they learned that one of the kidnappers had dropped a phone. It had disappeared. They did find the AK-47 that Abdur Rehman had reluctantly off-loaded.

Kiyani's big breakthrough came later that day.

He, along with his team, went to the home of Usman Basra to follow up on a lead. Basra wasn't there; his father and brother were. The agents convinced Basra's father to phone Basra and urge him to come home immediately. "Tell him it's an emergency," Kiyani instructed. Basra's father did as he was told, calling Basra, though not before the brother was able to text Basra and warn him the ISI were at the house, waiting for him. Fearing for his father's safety, Basra agreed to return.

What the ISI agents didn't know was that Basra was not at home because he was busy kidnapping me.

**My kidnappers took me to a safe house in a respectable** area of Lahore that they'd acquired anonymously through an intermediary. They knew that my kidnapping would set off a series of roadblocks and crackdowns, and it would be extremely hard to get me out of Lahore in the first twenty-four hours, so they'd decided to hide me until they had a chance to smuggle me out of the city. When Basra received the call from his father, he was at the safe house with me and the other abductors. He knew the ISI were waiting for him, but he also knew that they'd contacted him in relation to the Weinstein kidnapping, not knowing that he was deeply involved in mine.

Muhammad Ali urged Basra to stay, but Basra, concerned about his family and their safety, said that he had to return home. He was worried about the fate of his father and brother in the hands of the ISI. His strategy was to create a distraction long enough for Muhammad Ali to complete the second sequence of the plan, i.e., to transport me across the country to FATA (Federally Administered Tribal Areas), a treacherous part of Pakistan, a training center and breeding ground for lawless activities. What he didn't realize was that by turning himself in, he was also saving my life. All because of that phone he'd accidentally dropped.

When Basra returned to his father's home, the ISI quickly took him into custody. They were unable to find enough evidence to link him to the Weinstein kidnapping. He was minutes away from being released when the lost mobile phone was recovered. A major breakthrough for Colonel Kiyani, as this linked Basra directly to my abduction.

In the aftermath of my kidnapping, ISI agents had located a scrap retailer who had bought the cell phone from a municipal street cleaner. Once the ISI had recovered the phone, they set about tracing to whom it was registered. In Pakistan, every mobile phone must be registered using personal family contacts. When the agents investigated the contacts used to register this phone, it led them to a young woman who told them she'd helped get the phone for a student of her father's. That student had given them some story about a conflict with his own family and pleaded for their help.

Colonel Kiyani asked her what the student's name was.

"Usman."

"And where does he live?"

"In DHA," she said, naming a neighborhood in Lahore.

Kiyani's deputy, excited, whispered to him that the ISI had a man, Usman Basra, who lived in DHA, already in custody, in connection to the Weinstein case. And they were just about to set him free.

Colonel Kiyani asked the woman, "Are you talking about Usman Basra?"

"That's right. That's him."

The colonel couldn't believe his good fortune. This was a miraculous development. One of the main suspects in my kidnapping, a mystery man on a motorcycle, was sitting in ISI headquarters, already locked up.

**Returning to his office immediately, Colonel Kiyani had** Basra brought to him. Basra sat in a chair opposite the colonel's desk, expecting to be released. Instead, Kiyani asked him straightaway, "Are you involved in the kidnapping of Shahbaz Taseer?"

Basra took a moment, then leaned back in his chair with a smug smile and confidently confirmed it was too late:

"They've already gone."

After some interrogation, the colonel persuaded Basra to reveal the location of the safe house. Kiyani went with several officers and an extraction team early on Sunday morning to the safe house, in a respectable middle-class neighborhood in Lahore. They stormed the house and found it empty. Abandoned. All that was left was an old mattress, some discarded license plates, my broken sunglasses, a chair with shreds of rope hanging from it, and a syringe filled with what turned out to be, after they tested it, my blood.

Clearly, they had arrested the right man. With his help, they had found the right house. But my kidnappers knew they were coming and were already gone. And with them so was I.

# 8

I was kept for two days and nights in the safe house. Years later, I learned that this house was doors away from the home of my senior colleague Imran Hafeez. This was not some shantytown on the outskirts of the city; quite to the contrary, it was an upscale, newly developed housing estate, full of young professionals and their families, going about their daily business. Blissfully unaware of the criminal activities a doorstep away. Recently purchased through a cash transaction, the house held four violent men and one drugged hostage chained to the leg of a bed.

I was in and out of consciousness. The room was dark and dank. The air hung with the pungent smell of stale perspiration. The rancid odor, along with the panic, made me sick with fear.

Every so often, I'd wake up. I felt the same strange disorientation you have when you wake from a vivid dream. Along with panic, my first thought was always *Why am I wearing women's clothing?* The next: *Why can't I move?* It would take me a second to realize I was chained to a bed. The burka's eye-holes were covered with fine mesh, which made seeing diffi-cult, and the headpiece was twisted around so I could barely see out of it. The burka was made of synthetic material and the room was very hot. It felt like waking up in a grave. On more than one occasion, I woke up and thought I was already dead.

Then someone would beat me and drug me until I was out again.

**I was propped up in a chair and slapped awake.** My hood was off but I had a blindfold on.

"Don't worry," a voice kept saying. "All this will be over soon. You'll be home tomorrow."

I clung to those words. My family would pay the ransom, they would release me, and this would be wrapped up in one day. Maybe two.

I held on to this notion like a lifeline.

*One day. Maybe two.*

Then I was punched in the face and pumped full of keta-mine again.

**Though I didn't know this, since I'd been taken, my kidnap-**ping had become big news. By Saturday, reports were all over television about the abduction of Shahbaz Taseer, the son of the late Salmaan Taseer. There was more hype as my family is a part of the media cadre.

The amount of news coverage surprised my kidnappers. They'd thought of me, as my captor had said, as "a piece of treasure." All this attention led them to believe that they'd hit the jackpot. They began to think that, in taking the son of the famous Salmaan Taseer, they had a chance to deal a blow to the government of Pakistan. They thought they could use me to cripple the country.

If you think this delusion led them to treat me with greater reverence or care, you'd be mistaken. If anything, they became even more insane about what they might hope to get in exchange for my life. At first, they'd whispered to me that this was just a simple kidnapping, that I'd be home in a few days. Now, thanks to their newfound belief that I was some kind of national celebrity, the kidnapping had become something much more complicated and dangerous.

**Very early on Sunday morning, the day after Basra had** turned himself in to the ISI, my captors took me from the safe house in a different car from the one used in my abduction. I had been drugged so many times, and with such recklessness, that I'd overdosed and vomited all over the burka they had hidden me in. I felt sick, woozy, and disoriented. When one of my captors tried to feed me a piece of watermelon, I couldn't stomach it, thanks to the ketamine, and threw up bile all over the floor.

I'd repeatedly been beaten. I could barely stand. My clothes were covered in blood. To get me out of the city, I was again stuffed into the footwell behind the front seats of the car. Any utterance or movement by me elicited a violent kick.

I recall waking up and saying I had to urinate urgently. I sat up as best I could and saw we were on a main road heading out of Lahore. I knew right away this was bad. It meant we were on our way to who knew where. Afghanistan. Tajikistan. Some distant land beyond that.

Crouched in the back seat, wrapped in my disgusting burka, I felt a moment of galvanizing anger. "For God's sake," I shouted in the car, "stop and let me step outside to relieve myself!" I felt that a request to stop the car for a moment was not unreasonable.

My kidnappers disagreed. Someone punched me. Someone kicked me. Then one of my kidnappers took pity on me. He shoved a bottle at me. To piss in.

I started screaming incoherently, creating a ruckus, clearly hysterical; panic and fear had kicked in.

As I carried on, the driver turned and shouted over his shoulder, "I don't need this! Put him out!"

More ketamine.

**I remember we pulled up to one last army checkpoint, this** one on a highway far outside the city. I was awake, but barely. The ketamine was finally wearing off. I was in the burka again, sitting up, my head covered, squeezed between two men in the back seat. They knew that a woman in a burka would never speak to army officers at a checkpoint. And that the officers would never bother her.

As we pulled up to the checkpoint, one of the men at my arm pressed the tip of a knife to my side.

"If you speak, I will gut you," he said quietly. "I will kill you right here."

We pulled up to the stop.

I knew he would do it. Of that I was absolutely sure. Nothing about these men seemed rational, and they seemed to have little interest in self-preservation. They seemed ready to die and to take me with them. I could speak, I could call out for help, I could try to scramble from the car, but what then? These men might get arrested or shot, but I'd never know because I'd be dead, gutted in the back of the car.

I was sure of that.

An army officer looked over the car. He barely gave the back seat a glance.

Just a few men and a silent woman in a burka, heading out of the city. How the smell alone didn't alert him, I'll never understand.

He waved us on. We drove.

With that, we left Lahore behind us. My home disappeared in the rearview mirror.

We were on the highway now, heading away from the city, and on the road to a place I couldn't even imagine. We were likely headed toward the mountains in Afghanistan, beyond Pakistan's western border. Or maybe even somewhere farther still.

All I knew for certain is that we were going to a part of the world I'd never been in. To a place where men go to vanish, either by choice or by force.

# 9

**A**fter what seemed an endless painful journey, in and out of consciousness, I woke up in the room with the mud floor and the red bucket.

The room that would be my world for the next four and a half years.

Mostly, my captors ignored me, leaving me chained. I sat continuously hunched on the floor trying to piece together the puzzle of the nature of their demands. There was just frustrating silence.

On the morning of my first day, one of the guards brought me a cheap plastic lota, a pitcher-like vessel for washing oneself after using the toilet or, in my case, the red bucket. The guard put the lota down near my hands. The lota had water in it. I was crazed with thirst. Dehydrated, I gulped the entire pitcher. Holding the empty vessel up, I gestured for more.

I understood quickly that was my first big mistake.

The guard was short but well muscled, with a thick torso and a scraggly black beard, barely nineteen. The scarf had fallen, allowing me a glimpse of his teenage face. He wore a dirty *shalwar kameez*, a traditional Pakistani outfit. I was dressed in the same outfit, my office suit having long since been stripped away and left behind. This was to be my attire for the entire duration of my abduction.

My never having been deprived of something as basic as water brought home a new reality. I held the lota up to him; at first, he didn't understand. I asked him in Urdu, "*Ubu? Pani?*" Food? Water? Weak from hunger and fatigue, and nauseous from ketamine, I again asked for more water. He looked down at me, uncomprehending, then gave a snarled grin. Even though he spoke no Urdu, he pointed to the lota, then held up one finger.

I understood.

That was it. One lota's worth. This ration of water was meant for the whole day. And now it was gone.

The searing heat of August, one of the hottest months of the year in Pakistan, makes life unbearable. The windowless room was over one hundred degrees Fahrenheit. The allotment of water in my lota at the beginning of each day was to last me till sunrise the next morning. It was for *wuzu*, the ceremonial cleansing before prayer; for washing after using the toilet; and for drinking. There was barely enough water in the lota for any one of these, let alone all three. This unhygienic vessel was to be my only source of drinking water.

The guard left. He later brought me breakfast: a cup of sugarless black tea and a stale crust of bread on a plate. Treating me like a leper, he shoved the plate, from a distance, to where it rattled on the ground near my cuffed hands. I grabbed the food and lifted it awkwardly to my mouth. I gratefully drank the tea and gobbled the bread.

The remainder of the day was spent sitting, thirsty, hungry, desperate, and alone. I was terrified.

Memories of my happy home and family of just a few days earlier were flooding my thoughts. From a daily routine that revolved around work, family, and friends, it was now a life of solitary confinement, shackled to the floor, at the mercy of ruthless barbarians who had no appreciation for life as they had nothing to lose, willing to give their lives for some invisible cause.

My existence was starting to feel like a vivid dream that slowly dissipates once you wake up, until finally it slips away completely.

**This situation was entirely alien, causing me anxiety and** confusion as never before. I was exasperated and unable to help myself or bring about any sort of relief.

In this space there were zero options. No respite. If I was thirsty, I remained so. I stayed hungry, perspired profusely, was nauseous, and ached all over. I had an open cut over one eye. The mosquitoes buzzed and swarmed around me; I was unable to raise my hands to swat them. I sat like that and hours passed with me having no idea where I was, or what my captors wanted, or if I'd ever make it back to my world again.

I needed to find the strength to reconcile myself to these altogether new surroundings.

The diminishing light indicated sunset, followed by nightfall and the onset of my first night in my holding cell. I was left in pitch darkness. There was no electricity here, but the mud-walled structure cooled down slightly once the sun set.

Chained and barely able to move, I did my best to lie on the dirt floor. My body ached from the relentless beatings during the journey here. I tried to comfort myself with the straw pillow and sheet left near me in the room.

As I lay my head on the pillow, I realized that tiny white maggots were squirming in its straw. I wrapped the sheet around my head and slept as best I could.

That was the first day.

**To survive, I had to quickly adapt to my new surroundings,** mentally and physically, and concentrate on self-preservation. That meant confronting and accepting the reality of my situation and fighting every instinct that had been normal and natural to me in my life. I had to accept and understand that everything had changed.

This would include the absence of every person I held precious, every comfort I'd ever enjoyed, every advantage I'd taken for granted—all of that was gone.

I recall the feeling of the chains on my wrists in those first days, how they cut painfully into my skin. Not long ago, I thought, I'd been wearing a Bulgari on that same wrist. The contrast seemed absurd, beyond belief. I didn't care about losing my watch. I missed my family and my home. My cosseted life was a world of security, comfort, and privilege. My new life was chains, fear, pain, and solitude.

My life was now a series of unfortunate events with no clear end in sight.

Dawn of day two brought out a different person in me. I did not even fully realize it. But when I look back, I can see that, as soon as the second day began, I'd already started a journey. This journey would last for over four years. I discarded Shabby T and embraced Shahbaz Taseer, the person who would get me through. I'd learn to forget the luxuries and the amenities I had once enjoyed. I would find a will to fight for the real things of value I had lost. This will to keep fighting would sometimes fail me, but it would never abandon me. If I held on to it, it could keep my hope alive. It could keep *me* alive. But if I lost it, I was doomed.

**On the bright side, my captors were, at first, if not friendly,** then at least impersonal. The two guards who came in and out of the room said little to me, and when they did pay attention, it was usually to belittle or harass me in some derogatory way. It quickly became clear that I was nothing to them, a barnyard animal, a means to an end. If one of my kidnappers had called me "a piece of treasure," my new guards treated me like worthless trash. In their minds, they were true believers, righteous warriors in a holy war, and I was an infidel, a *kafir*, worse than garbage. I was valuable to them only as a cash cow.

But at least on the first day they didn't yet hate me or go out of their way to harm me. They hadn't grown irritated with the language barrier or begun to berate me constantly in frustration as they waited for instructions. They were as bored as I was; they viewed me just as one might look at a poor, sad soul lying in the street, or an animal struck or knocked down on the road. They couldn't spare a thought for me, much less mercy. At least, on the first day, they weren't tormenting me or hurting me for sport.

That came on the second day.

**I learned to ration the lota water and take a sip of the** breakfast tea and then let the tea go cold. That way, I could use the cold tea as additional water, either for drinking or to refill my lota. The bread was stale and nearly inedible, which is saying something when you're literally starving, but I consumed it anyway. Lunch on the second day consisted of a bowl of instant noodles. The only meal for the day. The first time they brought it, I ate the whole portion, slurping it hungrily from the bowl. Then I sat hungry until the evening, when I tried to sleep over the protests of my empty stomach.

I learned to split the Maggi noodles into two portions, one for lunch and one for later. I divided my portion carefully, clinging to my father's wisdom. Living as an impoverished student in London, he split in half his daily ration of a single fruit and nut chocolate bar to keep up his energy. Maggi noodles are far from a chocolate bar, but I divided them up in the same way. Thus I had something to eat in the evening, when the hunger became too constant to ignore.

Making portions to carry me through the day, I realized I'd often complained of being hungry in the past. You know that feeling: "I'm starving!" you protest. I'd said it myself a million times. But I'd never known actual hunger. Not like this. Now, hunger meant my body craving and demanding food, and being unable to move, let alone find food to feed myself. It was soul crushing. I would eat what I would get when my captors gave it to me and not before, and nothing more than that. The meager quantity was never near enough. I could no more escape my hunger than the heat or my chains.

The way countries manage their prisons reflects their minimum standard of humanity. Prisoners are entitled to basic amenities, such as running water, use of toilets, food, and human company. I had nothing. An inadequate amount of water and food, no social interaction. My guards had no interest in anything I had to say or do. They felt relieved of their responsibilities once the noodles and the water were left by my side every morning.

Being kidnapped in Pakistan means only one thing: a ransom has to be paid. If your family cannot pay for your return, the kidnappers don't simply drop you off by the side of the road with a shrug and a pat on the back. They make a horrible example in the most gruesome way possible, to send out a clear message to the next victim's family.

As I prayed that my family would be able to meet a possibly unreasonable demand, to save my life, my blood would run cold with fear and anxiety.

My situation was black-or-white—nothing in between. No one here cared enough to ease my discomfort or fear. I wallowed in filth, with a parched mouth and perpetual hunger.

I had two guards, whose names I'd learn later. The stubby one who'd bring my breakfast called himself Omar Turk. He was cruel, perverted, and took pleasure in beating me. This small man, with a misguided sense of authority, unlocked my chains and handed me a broom, indicating I should sweep the floor. As I stood up with aching wrists and a stiff body from lack of movement, I fumbled with the broom. Omar Turk was infuriated by my ineffective sweeping skills and berated and beat me. He had wanted to do this for a few days; now he had the perfect excuse to punish me. Terrified, I crouched and cowered but nothing would stop him.

That was Omar Turk. He was the lesser of the two evils.

**The other guard, Abdul Momin, was far worse than Turk.** Abdul Momin was odious. He needed no excuse to beat me. A psychopath, he beat me for sport and bullied me for entertainment. He spoke Pashto in broken sentences, enough for me to understand his story. Abdul Momin spent endless hours boasting crudely of the murders and carnage that made up his résumé. Claiming to be a Muscovite, he was now a fugitive with a trail of heinous crimes. He'd brutally killed a couple of Uzbek girls he believed to be prostitutes. The stories were embellished with gory details, which he reveled in.

Time stood still. My guards brought my meager rations and occasionally tormented me, but for the most part left me alone. For hours on end, chained, hunched, I sat in the room. I woke. I ate. I sat. I slept. This went on for a few more days. Then a week. I kept waiting for someone to come in and explain what was going to happen next. I waited for some kind of word. I waited to meet the leader of this operation, who could explain what was going on. The one who'd hissed in my face when I'd been blind under a hood, "I've come for you, Shahbaz." But I heard nothing. I kept waiting. No one arrived.

The sun sneaked through the crack in the roof, then disappeared. That was the extent of my day. The sun came. The sun vanished. I fell back into darkness. Another week passed.

I thought of my father. How he'd been in solitary confinement early in his life, as a political prisoner, in a Lahore jail. He was arrested for protesting against the military dictatorship of General Zia-ul-Haq, Pakistan's president at the time. I still missed my father fiercely. The protective umbrella that had shielded me was gone forever. I found myself alone. Abandoned.

The situation felt hopeless. My mind raced with unanswered questions. I would ask myself the same questions repeatedly: Was my family aware of where I was? Who were these people holding me? What organization did they belong to? And most important, what was their demand? Remembering my father's stories of incarceration and solitary confinement and how he had emerged a stronger person, I wondered if I would be the same or, indeed, if I would return at all.

All of these thoughts of my father's experience didn't make me feel closer to him, not at first. If anything, they brought me more despair. His was a story. He had been a prisoner of conscience, jailed because he'd fought for his ideals. I was a prisoner of circumstance. I'd been snatched against my will in broad daylight in the street because of my surname. I wasn't being held for having taken a principled stand or for protesting a brutal regime. I merely represented a lottery ticket. Nothing more. I could draw no respite or solace from my father's experiences of jail.

*There is no way I am strong enough to endure this.* This thought haunted me as I sat alone. *There is no way I am as strong as my father.*

I recalled that my father had told me as a child how he'd passed the days in solitary. Each day, he'd scratch a line in the wall. As a kid, when he told me, it sounded like a corny scene in an old-fashioned movie. But he convinced me it had helped him keep his sense of time. When you're locked away with no contact with anyone, it's easy to lose your perspective with the world, he explained. At least this way he knew days were passing, that life was moving on, and that one day his ordeal would end, even if, as each day passed, that end seemed as if it would never come.

I started doing the same thing. From my position, I could edge over and reach one wall. Luckily, the walls were made of mud, which was soft enough that I could scratch a faint mark in it with my thumbnail. I did my best to guess how many days I'd already been here. After that, I carefully gouged a new mark as each day passed.

"I am not made of a wood that burns easily," my father had famously written to my mother while he was held in the dungeons of the Lahore Fort jail, as a way to reassure her that he would return unscathed. As I sat alone in a cell of my own, one question plagued me:

*What kind of wood am I made of?*

I was too frightened to consider the answer.

# 10

The ensuing weeks remained uneventful, other than my being shifted to new accommodation within the structure. This gave me a better understanding of the compound, which included, other than my prison cell, a mini-headquarters referred to as the *markaz* and a bunker for transient mercenaries. Having had no interaction with any of them, I had no idea of what their mission was, where they came from, where they were going.

Surrounded by windowless walls, I could be compared to a blind man, depending solely on my senses. Listening carefully, I counted ten men in all; however, I was unable to follow their conversations owing to the language barrier.

Beyond my room, an adjoining courtyard led to a shower and the rudimentary toilets, a kitchen of sorts, and a separate room where the men slept. The location of the compound remained an enigma.

For the most part, Abdul Momin and Omar Turk were the only ones who checked in on me and brought my food. I was alone. I imagined the other men had better food than my black tea and stale bread. But why would they spare a thought for me, the *kafir* chained like an animal?

In my new surroundings was a small hole in the roof for heating. I tried to look at the sky through the hole, but the light hurt my eyes. Chained and tied to the floor, to combat the emptiness of endless hours in solitude, I decided to befriend my mind. The lyrics to all my favorite rap songs came to memory. Making a mental list of good friends and acquaintances, spanning my life all the way back to elementary school, I felt an involuntary smile when recalling some of our antics.

One day, I spotted a spider weaving a web on the ceiling. I named him Peter. I watched Peter work for hours in the rafters. Over time, we became friends.

He was my constant companion and confidant. Peter was a good listener. I told him about my life. I told him how much I missed my father. I recited Chris Rock comedy routines I had listened to so often they were committed to memory. Sometimes I would lie there silently watching as Peter weaved his web in the damp darkness of the ceiling. To my eyes, the web's patterns had some meaning that only Peter knew; perhaps I would unlock the cryptic message in his design. While he worked tirelessly, I gave him encouraging pep talks. "You can do it, Peter! Hang in there!" I'd say. Or I'd sing the "Spider-Man" theme to him. *Spider-Man, Spider-Man / Does whatever a spider can.*

In the evenings, as the sun faded, the mosquitoes descended through the hole. The sound of the mosquitoes, an incessant drone, began to haunt me. Peter and his delicate cobweb were my only protection from their onslaught. I rooted for Peter to build bigger, more intricate, more complex webs, complete with their elaborate hidden meanings. I cheered for Peter to snare every mosquito in the vicinity. He was my protector and I hoped that Peter, unlike me, was eating well.

**Allow me to give you a glimpse into those moments. I felt I** would go mad; I wondered if it had already happened. As the days meandered into weeks and eventually months, my mind became my enemy. I would cry in solitude. Planning for the future was clearly a meaningless indulgence. I could see no hope in the current situation. The same four walls, the same endless hours, the same uncertainty. It's both certain and uncertain: certain in that you know exactly what each dreary day will bring, and uncertain in that you can't know when or if it will ever end. Either thought will drive you mad if you dwell on it long enough.

So instead you start to dwell on the past.

You obsess over it. Every mistake, every conversation, every decision, every argument. You wonder what you did that brought you to a circumstance such as this. Now I've a clear understanding of hindsight. *If only I had listened to my wife. If I had adhered to my schedule in Dubai and not cut my trip short. I should have taken the SUV along with a guard to work!* Your mind starts to dwell on the what-ifs. I became the prosecutor and the accused in my own endless trial.

*You must have messed up big-time to end up here*, you tell yourself. And you believe it. Otherwise why would God have let this happen to you? How else can you explain it? You do your best to resist these conclusions. But they begin to sound convincing.

Soon you've gone from wishing you'd stayed in bed one

morning to regretting the entirety of your life. Every choice haunts you. You wish to go back and change it all. If the life you've led brought you to this windowless room, in the hands of these men, how can that life be defended?

All you do is judge yourself. And find yourself guilty.

Hindsight can be cruel, especially if you are judge, jury, and executioner.

I sat in darkness and thought of my brother Shehryar. When my father was assassinated, it felt as if the whole world were against us. We needed to present a strong face, but I confessed to him in private that with our father gone I didn't feel as secure or as confident anymore. I wasn't sure how to go on. My younger brother, the one whom I'd relied upon so much, said, "You and I . . . we're one. We're the same. As long as we're together, no one can break us." And I believed him.

On the night before my abduction, we got into an unpleasant altercation and a nasty verbal exchange. Afterward I'd knocked on the door of his room.

There was no answer, so I knocked again.

"I'm in the shower!" he shouted through the door. I went back to my room, thinking we'd sort it all out in the morning.

That was weeks ago.

I should have waited.

I should have stood there and told him I was sorry.

As I sat alone, I realized I was sorry for so many things.

The combination of heat, dust, and sweat had developed a fine layer of caked mud all over my body and matted hair. Limited movement and scarcity of water denied me the opportunity to wash myself. Despite many requests, I was denied this basic need. I pleaded and advanced an argument on religious grounds to no avail.

To distract myself from boredom, I began tracing lines in the dirt covering my arms. Eventually, Omar Turk noticed my artwork; taking pity on my lack of artistic talent, he gestured for me to follow him. We were leaving the room. I had no idea where this would lead to.

I obediently followed him to the adjacent courtyard. A communal bathroom was located off the courtyard. It took me some time to adjust to the strong morning light as I stumbled behind him. Turk had taken me the bathroom before, to unload the contents of my bucket. As I look back, the saddest part wasn't the bucket's smell, but my acceptance of the smell and not being repulsed by it. I realize now, I had already been dehumanized. Though I was living beside a bucket full of excrement, the stench no longer bothered me. I had become accustomed to it. The thought broke me and I began to sob.

**Usually, after Omar Turk had accompanied me to the bath**room to empty the bucket, he'd give me a rag to wipe the bucket out. It was my job to keep it clean.

On this day, Turk had taken me to the bathroom without the bucket. The bathroom was an open place beside a wall, with no barriers, stalls, or showerheads, just a drain in the floor and a pail of cold water. A charpoy, a local kind of bed with a wooden frame and rope netting, was placed upright vertically on the other side. I was given a tiny bar of soap, the only luxury I'd had in weeks. He pointed toward the tap. It took me a second before I understood. I couldn't believe it. He was going to let me take a shower. I started to quickly disrobe.

Then I paused, waiting for him to give me a little privacy. He just sneered and stared. His face told me what I needed to know: He wasn't going anywhere. I'd get my shower with him standing there, watching.

I doused myself with the frigid water, doing my best to scrub away weeks' worth of grime. There was no electricity in this mud building, and no hot running water either. I felt humiliated, standing there scrubbing, with Turk's watchful eyes on me, yet also grateful for a tiny measure of cleanliness. At the back of my mind, I was terrified that Omar Turk was having me undress in the shower room for a more violating purpose. My only experience with captivity was from watching movies, and I knew that shower rooms were notorious venues for all manner of despicable attacks. But Turk didn't move. He just watched me.

I put on the same dirty *shalwar kameez* I'd been wearing. He led me to my room and chained me to the floor once more. My skin felt slightly cleaner but I felt dirtier than before.

To sum up my first weeks, they were flooded with loneliness and fear. Neither one ever let up, not for a second. Every moment was the same, yet my plight held the promise that the next moment might also be the last. The only people I interacted with had made it abundantly clear they didn't care if I lived or died. I felt that Abdul Momin would be happy to hear that my family couldn't pay, so that, at his hands, I would meet the same fate as the girls in Moscow.

Could my family pay? Had they even been asked to? I still had no information. Nothing had been clarified. All I had was the faint glimmer of hope I remembered from the day I was kidnapped: *This will all be over in a day, maybe two.* Of course, it had now been weeks. Three weeks, maybe four. I had only my scratches on the wall to give me a sense of how much time had passed. But I knew that if they'd wanted to kill me, they'd have done it by now. Instead, they took the trouble to hide me here, wherever "here" was.

Occasionally, I heard the chirp of a cricket, and in the silence of that place, even a noise that gentle would startle me. How could crickets even survive here? I wondered. They seem far too gentle for a place this wild.

**Each day, I continued to scratch my faint mark. By now I** had thirty, maybe forty marks. I knew over a month had passed. It was well into October. The weather had cooled a bit. I'd still heard nothing, but I hoped word would come soon. Assuming we were still in, or near, Pakistan, I knew we were coming to the close of the rainy season.

Maybe six weeks into my captivity, they told me.

"He's coming," one of my guards said.

Who? I asked. Who?

Muhammad Ali, they said.

I had no idea who that was. Or that he was the architect of my capture. Or that we'd spend the next four and a half years together.

Then, one night, in darkness, he arrived.

# 11

In the middle of the night, they entered my room, which was pitch-dark. I couldn't see much as my eyes were adjusting to the flashlights. I was manhandled and pulled to my feet still in a daze from the commotion and fear.

My eyes focused, and I saw a group of men. They wore masks or scarves to hide their faces. One of them had nothing on his face. He stepped forward; I could see him clearly. His skin was deeply tanned. He was tall and menacing, with long black hair and a wispy, unkempt beard. He spoke in perfect Urdu, my mother tongue. These were the first complete sentences I'd heard in weeks. He conversed politely, at first, showing concern about how I was enjoying my stay: "How's everything? You need anything?"

I wasn't sure what to say. Need anything? How about a bath? A hot meal? A key to unlock these shackles? A ride home?

"Do you know who I am?"

That's when I recognized him. "I believe I saw you in

Lahore. You're the one who brought me here." I remembered his face as he directed the mercenaries who pulled me from the car. I recalled his presence as they whisked me away. I will never forget how violently he struck me, causing a gash above my eye.

*This must be Muhammad Ali*, I thought.

He denied it. "No, that's not me. You've confused me with someone else."

For all his certainty of himself as a leader of great virtue, a man who lived in the good graces of God, the first thing Muhammad Ali told me was a lie. I recognized him. I knew him. I had seen him that day in Lahore. And he denied to me who he was.

I would remind him of this lie many times over the next few years.

Having summed up and measured his prize, he left me in the room, but not before he looked me over, in my anguish and pain, and smiled. I'd never seen such a sinister smile. My guards had been cruel juveniles, acting like bullies. Psychotic, yes, but mostly sad and scared, and clearly emboldened by the power of their situation to torment a total stranger. They seemed pathetic more than frightening, and opportunistic more than evil.

*Perhaps I'm wrong*, I thought at the time, *but this man seems genuinely evil.*

Over the next four years, I'd learn my initial instincts were spot-on.

**After that brief encounter, I rarely saw him.** Occasionally, he'd come in to talk to me, usually to give me an update on what he considered his ingenious plan. He admitted his lie to me, claiming he wasn't ready to reveal himself as the master-mind. "I asked for you one day and they delivered you to me," he said, boasting arrogantly. It had taken him six weeks to arrive at this house because, to escape detection, the kidnappers had split up and traveled separately. He'd sent me on while he and a few others arrived via another route. He claimed to have walked a considerable part of this journey. In his sharing of all this information with me, I finally learned where I was.

I was in Pakistan. In a city called Mir Ali, in the federally administrated areas of North Waziristan, straddling the western border with Afghanistan, as the crow flies about three hundred miles from Lahore.

With my limited knowledge of the terrain, I was unclear whether to feel relief or alarm. Knowing I was still in my home country was reassuring, yet in many ways North Waziristan was as far from Lahore as the arctic circle. The local government is controlled by a mixed batch of rival tribes largely overseen by the Pakistani Taliban. Mir Ali, with a population of under one hundred thousand impoverished tribal people, is a war-torn town. To an unfamiliar visitor, Mir Ali resembled a medieval village, with a bustling market surrounded by mud-wall buildings amid ruins of old. You're as likely to see donkeys and carts as you are to see cars or trucks. A majority of its mud houses and mosques were destroyed during a 2007 military operation by Pakistan's army against the Afghan Taliban. What remains, by the Tochi River, in between distant mountains and around a crumbling central bazaar, is in a valley crawling with militias from all over the region. This unsavory cocktail includes Turks, Chechens, Bosnians, Egyptians, Syrians, Saudis, Iraqis, Nigerians, South Koreans, Central Asians, Russians, Pakistanis, Afghans, Kashmiris,

Burmese, and Uzbeks. All this made Mir Ali the perfect venue to secrete away a kidnapping victim such as myself, for an unspecified time.

The indigenous inhabitants are typically farmers and poor. Their lives and livelihoods depend on swearing allegiance to the Taliban. These peasants are pawns in an unending international war, and they live surrounded by some of the most ruthless men on earth.

This area was a breeding ground for multiple terrorist organizations such as al-Qaeda, ISIS, and the Pakistani and Afghan Taliban. Many terrorist attacks were hatched in this area. The porous border with Afghanistan allowed a stream of new recruits to assemble here.

But as to who was holding me, that still remained a mystery.

My father often spoke of having studied at the university of life, and to my horror, I was now being exposed to the university of terrorism.

Muhammad Ali would often sit in my room and tell tales about the latest squabbles between rival factions or new plans to launch deadly operations. The moral of all of these stories was the same: to demonstrate what a brilliant and masterful tactician Muhammad Ali was.

I found Muhammad Ali to be erratic, easily swayed by the last person who had his ear. A masochist, he sadistically enjoyed physically and mentally torturing me.

He manipulated people around him with his religious and moral rhetoric, so that they would gladly lay down their lives for his cause. He claimed to be a religious follower of Islam, but was in fact a cult leader. He could recite Quranic verses verbatim but had no understanding of the words. His sadly perverse translation had little to do with the true meaning and spirit of Islam. He had a disarming wit and sense of humor that softened the monster inside him. To me, though, he only revealed the monster.

He would often visit me for an hour or so and pull up a stool to hold court. I soon learned he considered himself a strategist and the next big name in the ongoing jihad against the infidels. He outwardly appeared deeply devout, shaming me for hours about my allegedly sinful life.

He would carry an old laptop and show me video clips of his previous abducted victims, screening the clips with great pride. These disturbing videos often ended with a graphic beheading. He mentioned he had held a young man for almost four months, waiting for an agreed-upon ransom that never came, before executing him. In another case, they'd kidnapped a businessman and succeeded in claiming a $1 million ransom from his family. After the success of that kidnapping, Muhammad Ali had convinced his superiors to let him use some of that money to fund a more ambitious kidnapping. This time, he promised, he would deliver someone of national prominence. He would kidnap one of the sons of the assassinated governor Salmaan Taseer.

For Muhammad Ali, I was his crowning glory and his ticket to the big leagues.

As we spoke, I tried to figure out which group exactly had taken me. In most cases abduction off the streets of a large Pakistani city means you've been taken by the Tehreek-e-Taliban or by affiliates of al-Qaeda. The Afghan Taliban did not engage in kidnapping for ransom, and ISIS, while a growing influence, did not operate so far into Pakistan. The Tehreek-e-Taliban and al-Qaeda lacked any formal structure and were open to new recruits and factions operating under their patronage.

Muhammad Ali and the gang that had taken me worked independently. They were part of a very different organization, established and known for its barbaric methods.

**After months of instant noodles, I began to lay out a strategy** in my mind to try to force a change to my meal plan. Clearly, begging for something different would yield no positive result. Weighing my options, considering every angle, every possibility, I came up with a devious plan that could provide food fit for human consumption. In the worst case, if it backfired, there would be more beatings.

The plan kicked off with occasional complaints of feeling weak and suffering from chronic headaches. "My family has a history of diabetes," I'd say if ever a guard showed even a moment of interest in my ailments. "I have to eat something different or I'll get sick." I hoped this would get Muhammad Ali's attention. After all, a sickly prisoner is more trouble than he is worth, and I still assumed Muhammad Ali wanted me alive, to cash me in.

After several conversations, a guard alerted Muhammad Ali. I told him what was wrong, about the diabetes.

Upon hearing of my ailment, Muhammad Ali smiled. "If this dog has diabetes, let's really give him something that will kill him and take him off our hands quick."

He dispatched the guard to get me a serving of rancid goat fat on a slice of bread.

Thus began a horrible new regimen. In place of noodles, I was dished out a serving of goat fat and bread every day. The sight and smell turned my stomach. I nibbled on the bread and tossed the fat into my toilet bucket.

Some days later, the uneaten goat fat clogged the guards'

toilet. Upon discovering this, Muhammad Ali was infuriated. In a cold and menacing way, he ordered me to eat some goat fat immediately. I pleaded and said I'd gag.

Muhammad Ali not only made me eat it, he decreed that if the goat fat was ever recovered from my waste bucket again, I'd eat it in the condition it was found.

I ate goat fat every day after that for over six months.

**Initially when Muhammad Ali visited me, he skillfully wore** me down with his mind games. What's more, he enjoyed it. He would talk about my siblings and how they were cheating me. How they were scheming to take over the business or steal our home from us. The worst for me, though, was when he'd simply say that my family had forgotten me. I knew in my heart that it couldn't be true, but in my head, I wondered if it was.

The endless hours of loneliness ate at me. My only human contact was with men who despised and berated me. I had no one to comfort or reassure me, no sign at all that anyone I'd left behind still cared. *They could be dead for all I know*, I thought, *just like my father is*. He'd been murdered just a few months earlier by a religious fanatic. Now I'd been cast into this forsaken hellhole. How could I believe that any of the people I loved had been spared?

In my darkest moments, I started to think, *Why should I believe they still spare a thought for me at all.*

**Death preoccupied my mind. I considered putting an end** to this misery and taking my life. I wondered if choking myself with my chains was possible. I wrapped them around my neck and pulled tight, testing to see if I could go through with it. I couldn't. I felt worse, alone and a coward, unable to end my torment. My self-preservation took over, not allowing me to inflict irrational harm, only elevating Muhammad Ali's authority over me. Perhaps he was right, I thought. Either way, I felt dejected and a failure.

# 12

**M**y family had not forgotten me.

They were safe in Lahore, anxious, afraid, and frustrated. They learned that the ISI had discovered the safe house hours after I had left, finding my broken sunglasses, some bloody ropes, and a used syringe.

My family hadn't heard yet from the kidnappers. No ransom demands. No updates. No threats. Nothing. No idea as to who had taken me.

The silence continued for days. Then weeks. Then a month.

My mother was despondent but strong; after all, she had been through this once before. In the beginning of her marriage to my father, in her early twenties, he had been arrested and taken to the Lahore Fort, a notorious jail. She'd known where he was but got little word about his condition or when he might be released. She learned to be patient. She learned to carry on with her regular life each day, while never letting my father stray far from her mind.

There's a photo I cherish of my father emerging from Faisalabad Jail after four months in solitary confinement to greet me, his toddler son. In the photo, I look so happy to see my abba, unaware of what he had gone through. I thought of that photo a lot during my own captivity. The relief on my father's face and the happiness on mine. I wondered if I would ever get to feel those emotions, the joy that comes from regaining your freedom and once again holding your loved ones in your arms.

It's the strangest thing to have a loved one kidnapped. It is so open-ended. You miss them but you can't mourn them. They may come home tomorrow or never at all. You need to learn to live with that uncertainty. Every time your cell phone rings, you scramble to answer it while dreading what news it may bring.

Because of her previous experiences, my mother knew the lack of news about me was not good. My whole family understood that in most kidnappings the first forty-eight hours are crucial. This window of time can be the difference between a successfully resolved kidnapping, in which a captive is rescued or returned alive for ransom, and a botched operation that ends in the captive being killed or simply disappearing. The ISI had held out hope that they could still catch my kidnappers even though they'd slipped out of the city. Everyone understood that, once the kidnappers had escaped Lahore, I could be anywhere. There was little chance the ISI could find me, and even if they did, there was virtually no chance they could rescue me. All everyone could do now was wait.

So, they waited. Two days. Three days. A week. Then more.

In the meantime, the Pakistani media had a field day with my situation. The most outrageous rumors and speculation circulated. My kidnapping was connected to my father's killing, they claimed. No, actually the kidnapping had been staged. I was hiding out somewhere on the run from a business debt or a family squabble. In the absence of real information, rumors ran rife and the internet was aflame with lies. The reality was, no one knew anything, not even me. All I knew was that I was in a room somewhere with no idea where. My family knew even less than that.

**Another week went by. Then another. The news cycle** moved on. The internet was awash with other things to speak of. Soon a month had passed. Still no news for them.

I hate to imagine what those weeks were like for my family, for Shehryar and Shehrbano, my brother and sister, for my grandmother Amy, my *khala* Tammy and my *mamoo* Ehsan, my wife, and of course my mother. Imagine that, every time the phone rings or a new email arrives, you answer it or open it with dread, wondering if this will finally be the one that carries some news, and whether that news will be good or crushing. Wondering each time if the message will be a demand for money or simply a video of your loved one being slaughtered.

They waited. Another week passed. Another month.

Nothing.

Then, one day, Maheen got an email on her phone. She didn't recognize the sender's address.

She sent for my mother and opened the email.

It was a link to a video.

**I'd been in captivity for about two months. I'd come to** expect the routine beatings from the guards and the sporadic visits from Muhammad Ali. He loved to boast of how he'd plotted to snatch me off the streets and, just like that, here I was. He thought he was a tactical genius. These sessions were excruciating for me but at least they broke up the solitude. The rest of my days were spent in loneliness, fending off insanity.

One day, Muhammad Ali arrived with a different message. It was time, he'd decided, to contact my family.

I couldn't believe it. I was ecstatic. I could barely control my excitement. Maybe this was the beginning of the end. I'd finally get to speak to my mother, get to hear her voice for the first time in months. This madman would reveal his demands to my family and they would happily pay him, and I'd finally be on my way home. It was surreal, impossible to believe.

I shouldn't have believed it. Muhammad Ali soon explained to me what would happen. We weren't making a phone call. Not yet. We'd be making a video. Muhammad Ali had prepared what I was meant to read.

Two of his men came in carrying a video camera and a tripod. It was an impressively high-tech HD camera.

*Bloody hell*, I thought, *I'm going to get my head cut off in HD.*

They sat me up in my chains on a chair. They put me in a suicide vest. About twelve of Muhammad Ali's fighters came into the room, their faces covered by scarves. They stood behind me, a show of force. My silent, anonymous abductors.

While I was discouraged when I found out I wouldn't get to talk to my family or hear their voices, this felt like progress. There was still a glimmer of hope. This was the first step toward the endgame. Finally, I had a chance to send a message to my family to let them know I was alive, to reassure them that they should not give up on me, and to let them know there was still a way to bring me home.

Muhammad Ali handed me the sheet of paper. I glanced over the words and my heart sank.

The note was addressed to the president and the prime minister of Pakistan, not to my family. The speech was just lines of angry boasting and gibberish about how my abduction proved how strong Muhammad Ali's group was, how he could bring Pakistan to its knees. Nothing about ransom, no demands, no instructions. I would simply sit there and recite this ridiculous message, a mouthpiece for their propaganda.

As I scanned the message, I felt an urge to laugh. Muhammad Ali's ludicrous assumption that the government of Pakistan had shuddered to a halt because I had been kidnapped was absurd, and I knew it. My family cared enough about me to do anything to bring me home. I doubted the same was true of the country's government.

The red light came on, indicating the recording had begun. I did as I'd been told. I read out the statement. We recorded the video once in English and once in Urdu. When we were done, I looked at Muhammad Ali and asked if it was okay. It must have been because his men dismantled the tripod and took the equipment from the room.

My mother contacted Colonel Kiyani right away. The email didn't contain the video, but it contained a link to a website where they could download it, along with a password to access the file. They were concerned about blindly following this link, but anxious to see if it contained news. Gathering around my mother's desk, they clicked to download the video.

The image of me in a chair, chained, was crisp and clear. My beard had grown and my hair was straggly. Behind me was a row of anonymous men, their faces covered by scarves and their hands clasped in front of them. One of the men was identified as the one who'd lost his thumb. The intelligence agencies had seen this kind of video before, in which an extremist group showcases their captive and makes their outlandish demands. Except in this video, only I was speaking, reading from a written script. The video gave no clues as to my location or demands for my release.

Colonel Kiyani noticed something. I read the statement in Urdu, but I seemed to look up at someone just off camera and say "Okay?" in English. As if I was asking if I'd performed correctly.

He thought this over. If I was reading in Urdu, but saying "Okay?" to someone in English, that possibly meant my captors weren't native Urdu speakers. Which meant that even if they were holding me somewhere in Pashtun-controlled Waziristan, my captors were not Pashtuns.

There were other telltale signs. My mother picked up on the attire of the men standing behind me. Their clothes were worn loose, which isn't the style of the Pashtuns, who wear their *shalwar* bound tightly at the ankle. These two clues indicated it was not the Tehreek-e-Taliban who had kidnapped me, which is what everyone had been assuming. It was someone else, not from that region.

This, they realized, might not be good news.

**After we filmed the video, Muhammad Ali left me alone. It** was October, and the weather starting to turn colder. I was being held in the second place since I'd been kidnapped. My roommate and companion, Peter the spider, had long since disappeared. After weeks of waiting for some news, Muhammad Ali had offered me hope only to snuff it out.

Perhaps this was the start of a negotiation. A message to

my family that I was alive. That I was worth fighting for. We might still be reunited.

If I'd known then what my family knew, I might not have been so optimistic.

The intelligence agencies met with them to watch the video and laid out their concerns and observations. A primary one was that these were not native Pakistanis, therefore not part of the Taliban, and the agencies had no control over them. Usman Basra, in custody, had disclosed the identity of this group.

Colonel Kiyani confirmed, "These aren't Pashtuns. They are Uzbeks." The ISI suspected my kidnappers were part of the Islamic Movement of Uzbekistan, or IMU, a group already known to them. The IMU was one of the many terror groups that had taken refuge and gained a foothold in the lawless tribal lands that stretch along the Pakistani border with Afghanistan. Their goal is a fundamentalist Islamic regime in Uzbekistan, a former Soviet republic struggling to find its footing in the modern world. Colonel Kiyani offered further evidence for this conclusion. The masked soldier behind me who had a mangled hand and was missing a thumb. These injuries identified him as an IMU operative that the ISI already had a file on.

Colonel Kiyani had more disturbing news for my mother. He confided that, in the ISI's experience, the Uzbeks were among the cruelest of all the extremists, known for their penchant for violence. My mother's blood ran cold. My family had assumed they were dealing with the Afghan Taliban, al-Qaeda, or Tehreek-e-Taliban, groups they were confident they could negotiate with. The Uzbek terrorists are known for their brutality; it's a trademark.

Having finally heard word of where I was and seen proof

I was still alive, my mother shared the news with my siblings, but not that my captors were notorious for being merciless. They'd all just have to wait for the next video and hope it contained some actual demands, some key to bringing me home.

# 13

Once the first video was sent, Muhammad Ali would occasionally check on me. I'd complain to him about my conditions and plead for a chance to take a shower or shave my unkempt beard. He felt I was starting to blend in and look more like the men around me. The similarities would make it easier to hide me when I was transported from safe house to safe house. In my mind, it was as if my surroundings were a kind of cocoon and I was undergoing a slow metamorphosis. My outward appearance began to feel less like me.

After weeks of begging, my request finally had an effect. Muhammad Ali instructed a guard to give me a straight-razor blade so I could shave my body and my underarm hair. This was part of the traditional cleansing ritual, the *wuzu*, to prepare for daily prayer. "You're not a Muslim," Mohammad Ali told me, "but you think you're a Muslim, so you might as well act like one."

His rationale was grimly hilarious. They considered me a *kafir*, an infidel, and relished the pleasure of reminding me of that every day. Muhammad Ali would taunt me with the belief that my father was burning in hell. My captors barely gave me enough water to drink, let alone to spend on cleansing myself. Yet they still wanted to give me a chance to observe all the rituals and practices laid out in the Quran, which I had read at a young age, tutored by a local religious scholar.

A young Kazakh guard brought me the razor. He set down a bowl of water and a single, naked razor blade and left me alone.

I held the blade flat in my hand with trepidation.

As I looked at it, I considered that it might be put to another use.

In the dark quiet of that room the blade almost seemed to whisper to me.

I was about three months into my ordeal. The constant degradation at the hands of the guards had begun to wear me down. Muhammad Ali's formula to break my spirit—that I was a worthless, despicable figure who deserved only derision and scorn—was having the intended effect. I could only bolster my own morale for so long. The loneliness and diminishing hope had become almost too much to bear. Maybe it *was* too much, I thought, as I looked down at the razor blade and felt its slight weight on the palm of my hand.

In the quiet hours, questions plagued me. Would I ever see my family again? Or was I fated to endure these same miserable hours and days and nights until Muhammad Ali decided to kill me? Wasn't that how this would inevitably play out?

With thoughts like these wrapping their dark tentacles around my mind, the blade didn't represent death to me. It represented release. It was starting to seem like the last hope for escape that I might have.

But I also knew that this way out would not take me home

to my family. Nor would it transport me magically to my former life.

I began to drown in my shame. Imagine if my father could see me now. What would he say? When he faced a similar imprisonment, he had emerged a stronger, more resolute man, yet even that thought failed to bolster me. Instead, it felt like an anchor, pulling me down deeper into an abyss. Here I was, so broken, so desperate, when my father had endured so much. Was I made of the same wood as my father? Or did I burn easily?

Negative and morbid thoughts took over, anxiety set in, and I would find myself spiraling out of control. *I'm a worthless failure. No one will miss me when I'm gone.*

Pinching the blade between my fingertips, I raised it to my throat. It was an awkward moment. I felt defeated. Unable to face the possibility of taking my own life, despondent, I set the blade aside.

Upon reflection, it remains unclear to me whether I put it aside out of fear and weakness, or because of a modicum of inner strength that I felt in that moment. My captors would constantly berate me; my family and friends were nowhere. I was completely alone. I was lost.

But as I looked at the discarded blade, I realized, *I have no idea how this will end, but it will not end like this.*

*Not now, anyway.*

*Not yet.*

I began to understand Muhammad Ali's psyche. This was his ethos. This was how he controlled his little world, through fear and mind games.

He gave me the blade to torment me. These were his tactics in giving me the blade, on the pretense of helping me fulfill my religious obligations, to push me toward picking up the Quran. It was the one book Muhammad Ali would leave for me and allow me to read. He'd often mock me for my lack of knowledge, and since he had trained in a religious school, a madrassa, since he was a boy, he enjoyed lording his religious education over me. He would rattle on for hours about his great pious superiority.

In Pakistan, a compulsory subject in school is religious studies. I learned enough to get by. Celebrating religious festivals was a family affair and always a happy time.

I started, for the first time in my life, reading the Quran seriously. Muhammad Ali had left me one written in Arabic with an English translation at the bottom of each page, which meant I could read it right away, while also familiarizing myself with Arabic. The Arabic text was close enough to Urdu that soon it was legible.

At first, I read simply to pass time and in the hope of pleasing my captors. As I read, though, I realized that the Quran offered me three things. First, the scriptures helped me deal with my suicidal feelings, as the Quran forbids suicide, something religious extremists neglect to mention when they're convincing a young follower to be fitted with a suicide vest. Suicide out of despair of God's mercy is strictly forbidden, says the Quran. I took this to mean that if I killed myself, I'd be condemned to hell, which, believe it or not, I still thought would likely be slightly worse than where I was already. I'd be damned to an eternity trapped with madmen like Muhammad Ali.

So I put my suicidal thoughts aside. At least here, in this room, alive, there was still a glimmer of hope that I might see my family again. If I took my life, that chance would vanish. The only difference between hell and the room where I was, I realized, was that at least in this room I had hope. Perhaps

I was too optimistic, but the writing in the Quran gave me guidance, solace, and a reason to hold on.

Second, the Quran gave me hope. If you believe in God, I read, you cannot be hopeless, for God is hope. To renounce hope is to renounce God. These are the words of the Quran. Still, I questioned why God had chosen to put me in such a treacherous position with such twisted people. But I was open to this message. I need not fear these barbarians.

That's the final thing the Quran gave me, and it's likely the last thing Muhammad Ali expected when he berated me for not reading it. As I studied, day after day, page after page, I began to realize something. I'd spent my whole life ignoring God, but maybe I should have feared God after all, and in fearing God, I need not fear any man. Definitely not Muhammad Ali.

That's the invaluable gift the Quran gave me: A way past my fear.

The weeks grew colder. We were well into winter. I'd been in captivity nearly four months. I knew that from the marks I'd left on the mud wall of my cell.

As we got closer to the year's end, I thought often of Christmas, a particularly festive time in my home. I closed my eyes and tried to recall the smells and tastes of it. I imagined I was at my friend Rafael's house in Lahore, in the courtyard that had always been a stage for me, an arena, a coliseum, a place for me to perform for all my friends. I had enormous approval from family and friends for being an entertainer. The plants and flowers in that courtyard are reliably kissed by morning dew, and they shimmer in the winter sun. At Christmas, the tables are beautifully laid with the most delicious dishes. A perfect golden-brown turkey. A fragrant leg of lamb. Guava crumble! As I sat silently, alone, eyes closed, it was almost as if I were there. I could see it all in my mind's eye. Khurshid, Rafael's cook, had really outdone himself this year.

"Don't give Shahbaz the mic!" my friend Rakae shouts loudly. He was all too familiar with my affinity for performing, with little or no encouragement.

I take a sip of water and remove my sunglasses. This will be the Shabby T special they will talk about for years. I feel like Maximus Decimus Meridius from the film *Gladiator*. I want to point my sword toward the galleries and yell, "Are you not entertained?!"

"Take the mic away from him!" pleads Rakae again. He's got a new girlfriend who really does not need a five-minute highlight reel of his greatest high school adventures.

*Or does she?* I think mischievously.

"To repay the trust you all have bestowed in me over the years as the master of ceremonies, I shall begin today's games with our very favorite prey . . . Rakae!" I walk over to him, beaming with pride at my serendipitous rhyme. I can see him shrinking in my approaching shadow. "Did you know that Rakae lost his virginity—"

He tackles me and tries to wrestle away the microphone.

The laughter crashes in waves all around me. This is just the beginning of something beautiful. Rakae is the first in a long line of intended victims. The others may be laughing now, but they won't be when it's their turn to be my mark. As I sit with my eyes closed, I try to raise my hand to point out my next victim and . . . Clink.

I couldn't raise my hand.

I opened my eyes.

I was still there, in that room, bound by rusted chains.

As winter's bitter cold set in and the days became shorter,

as I sat in chains and darkness pensively wondering when Christmas would come if it hadn't already passed, Muhammad Ali paid me a visit.

"Come on. Time to make another video."

In my last leading role, I'd been seated, dressed in a suicide vest with a row of faceless men standing behind me. I'd read from a prepared statement addressed to the president and the prime minister of Pakistan. There'd been no mention of ransom or any demands.

Muhammad Ali coldly turned to me and in measured words informed me I would be speaking directly to my family.

My heart raced with excitement. I was almost light-headed with anticipation, naively thinking this was the first step toward the home stretch.

Nearly half a year of my life had been snatched, lost in a hell I could never have imagined. It wasn't that my family was failing to meet the demands. They had no idea what the demands were.

Now they would know, and that would, I believed, start the process to bring me home. To "inspire" me, Muhammad Ali opened his laptop and showed me a few videos of his last captive, a young man from Lahore whose family had been unable to meet the required ransom. He showed me the man being tortured, hung by his arms and beaten with chains. To show their seriousness they sliced off his thumbs, which Muhammad Ali told me they sent in a package to his family. In the final video, the man kneels and begs, crying, calling out to Allah for mercy. Cool, collected, and psychotically calm, Muhammad Ali severed the man's neck with a large serrated knife. It was the bloodiest and most unholy act I had ever witnessed. I felt sick. I felt pain for this poor man. Unprecedented levels of anxiety took over me. My mind drew parallels to the Daniel Pearl execution. These people were ruthless and would go to any lengths.

Muhammad Ali closed the laptop. This, he promised, was what awaited me if my family failed to meet their demands. I had no reason to doubt him. After all, he had done it before. Until now, the thought that my family could not save me had not crossed my mind.

I was led onto a nondescript veranda, primarily used for prayer. He squared me up to face the camera. He handed me a sheet of paper that detailed their demands. I was strategically placed on a chair, allowing the men to stand behind me while I faced the camera. As I nervously focused, my heart skipped a beat. I was numb and breathless. Disturbingly, what I read led me to believe I would never, ever make it home alive.

# 14

In my chair, I started to have what could only be called a panic attack. I went over and over their demands.

"You've brought me here to kill me!" I shrieked hysterically, frantically, at Muhammad Ali.

"Calm down. They will pay."

"This is not a real demand!" I said, desperate.

"I've broken the government!" He was getting worked up. "I've humiliated them by snatching you!"

"Trust me," I replied, trying unsuccessfully to calm myself. "I deal with governments and contracts all the time. No one is going to pay this amount. It's impossible."

In all my conversations before with Muhammad Ali, I had attempted to be civil. I hated him, despised his face, and trembled when I heard his approach. But I was his prisoner, his pawn. I knew very well my life lay in his hands. I had never yelled at him, never even raised my voice. I had always been pliant and obedient.

*Jee bhai, jee bhai*—if only out of self-preservation.

None of that seemed to matter anymore.

"This is insane," I shouted. "You're a lunatic."

He seemed legitimately taken aback by my protests. I assumed he thought he'd lead me here and I'd deliver his demands like a cowering captive. Instead, I was having a meltdown and calling him a lunatic to his face.

"Calm down!" he yelled back. "They will pay!"

But I knew they would not. No one could.

What he was asking was impossible. Which meant I was as good as dead.


**My mother, who was leading the effort to bring me home,** became concerned about my siblings and my wife. One day in November, she sat them down.

"I know how hard this is for you," she said. "Imagine what Shahbaz is going through. We have to be strong for him. He is out there, alive. He'd want to know that you're okay. I'm sure he thinks of you every day. And he will be back. You have to believe that. And you need to stay strong so you're ready for that day."

My mother had reached out to a well-known hostage consultant, Jamil Yousaf. He was a successful businessman based in Karachi who'd become a prominent expert vigilante on resolving kidnappings. By the time my mother contacted him, Jamil Yousaf, who was then in his midsixties, was well-known across Pakistan for having resolved multiple kidnappings. In some cases, the ransom was delivered and the captive was returned unharmed. In other cases, the victims had been rescued.

Jamil Yousaf had flown to Lahore shortly after my kidnapping to meet with my mother and my aunt Tammy to help tutor them in dealing with the kidnappers. "When you speak with the kidnappers, document every word," he instructed my mother, because he knew that during these stressful phone calls, people's minds would naturally go blank. He suggested she establish code names for each person involved in the negotiations, so she could always be sure of whom she was talking to. He encouraged her to negotiate with the kidnappers directly, in an effort to prolong her contact with them and help humanize herself and me in the kidnappers' eyes. In his experience, kidnappings for ransom were usually resolved in just a few months, as techniques to track kidnappers had become more sophisticated and consultants such as Jamil Yousaf had been more successful in extracting captives alive. Most kidnappers were not ruthless killers; they just wanted to cash out as quickly as possible.

But, he admitted to my mother, his expertise lay mostly in dealing with groups of thugs or cells of al-Qaeda. He'd started out as a kidnapping resolution consultant by studying the methods of Karachi's many criminal gangs. He had no experience dealing with Uzbek extremists, he confessed. With no demands and little information, he offered generic advice and guided my mother on how to proceed. It was possible, he warned her, that his tactics would have no effect on them at all.

So my family waited.

My mother, despite being home and comfortable in her surroundings with a strong support group of friends and family, was indirectly a prisoner too, powerless, alone, desperate, entirely at Muhammad Ali's mercy.


**It took twelve takes to complete this new video. The objec**tive for me was to remain calm but terrified. I, however, knowing these demands were unrealistic, was overwrought with emotion. I kept breaking down, unable to deliver the desired emotion of the message.

I'd spent many months envisaging multiple scenarios, playing them out in my mind, as to what the demands on my family would be. I held the paper with trepidation, getting my first glimpse as to what could be my ticket to freedom, which read out more like a death sentence.

Muhammad Ali was demanding an unprecedented amount, 4 billion rupees, and the release of nearly thirty detainees, ranging from infamous terrorists to his personal accomplices, men such as Usman Basra, who'd been caught and arrested during my kidnapping. To add insult to injury, the name at the top of the list was Mumtaz Qadri, the man who had murdered my father.

It was a two-tier demand.

First, the money.

I had assumed he would ask for something in the range of four hundred thousand U.S. dollars, a fairly typical ransom in keeping with more recent demands. The 2008 global meltdown had hit our family business, as it had affected many businesses around the world. My father had worked tirelessly to rebuild and steady his own. His assassination in early 2011 had a negative impact and our business faltered again. Using out-of-the-box solutions, we'd managed to restore a semblance of order, bringing profit to our companies again.

I was confident my family could raise a few hundred thousand dollars if it meant bringing me home alive.

This demand of 4 billion rupees was not a few hundred thousand dollars.

It was roughly equivalent to 45 million U.S. dollars.

I knew there was no way my family or anyone else could

pay that sum for my release. This meant that I was as good as dead.

When I said this to him, Muhammad Ali tried to school me on the art of negotiation. He considered himself a savvy dealmaker. If he asked for $45 million, they would give him $10 million, he explained.

Ten million, 40 million, 50 million—what difference did it make? "You might as well ask for a hundred million, or a billion dollars," I yelled hysterically, believing I had nothing to lose. I knew it didn't matter what the exact figure was. Forty-five million dollars was unrealistic and beyond my family's capacity to pay. It didn't matter what the numerical figure was. The fundamental problem was not his outlandish demands, but his delusional belief that the Pakistani government would move heaven and earth to secure my release. That was not even a remote possibility.

The second tier was the list of men.

I didn't recognize most of the names, but I could see this wish list, full of terrorists and criminals, would be impossible to fulfill. That my father's killer was the first name on the list only drove the dagger in deeper. Whether from the intense media attention in the days after my kidnapping or from Muhammad Ali's deranged misconception, he'd forged the idea that I was the greatest prize in all of Pakistan.

Knowing this to be untrue and far from reality, I knew my family would go to any lengths to secure my freedom. However, I was well aware that even $10 million in cash was a stretch. Securing the release of a few dozen most-wanted terrorists would be impossible. Muhammad Ali had miscalculated the extent to which the Pakistani government cared about my fate.

Crippled with fear, I had to face a video camera and relay

the demands to my family. I knew that I was simply reading out my death sentence.

As we recorded take after take, I was unable to deliver the desired emotion on camera, and this ordeal continued endlessly. These reckless demands, I believed, would not lead to a positive conclusion.

This was the end of my life. That was clear to me.

Now, the only unanswered question was when and how painful and agonizing the end would be.

# 15

There is a prayer in Islam called the Ayat al-Kursi, which is recited by Muslims as a prayer of protection. It translates from the Arabic text like this:

> *In the name of Allah, the Beneficial, the Merciful.*
> *Allah! There is no God but He,*
> *the Living, the Self-Subsisting the Eternal.*
> *No slumber can seize Him, nor sleep.*
> *His are all things in the heavens and on earth.*
> *Who could intercede in His presence without His*
>     *permission?*
> *He knows what appears in front of and behind His*
>     *creatures.*
> *Nor can they encompass any knowledge of Him except*
>     *what He wills.*
> *His throne extends over the heavens and the earth,*
> *and He feels no fatigue in guarding and preserving them,*
> *for He is the Highest and Most Exalted.*

The purpose of the prayer is to call down angels to protect you. Physical copies of the prayer are a common talisman in Pakistan. Like many Muslims, my father wore this prayer on a chain around his neck, inscribed on a tiny round of silver. I could remember seeing it dangling there and asking him what it meant. I couldn't read it in the original Arabic script, hence I never truly grasped its meaning. Alone in darkness and captivity where time was slow, I reached out to Allah to answer this prayer for my protection.

In solitude, I took a step toward faith and learned the words by heart, hoping they would shield me.

I recited the prayer daily, and this tonic gave me strength.

Each time I recited the verse, I thought of my father. I remembered how much he had cherished his necklace. My own captors referred to him disparagingly as an infidel, viciously claiming he was burning in hell and that I would soon join him.

*No slumber can seize Him, nor sleep.*
*His are all things in the heavens and on earth.*

As I read my Quran daily, I noticed that the Allah I was reading about in the Holy Scripture bore little resemblance to the one that my captors loved to go on and on about. The Allah I found in my Quran is a merciful God, he protects those who are true to him. He also demands that his followers be moral, noble, and even-tempered. My captor, Muhammad Ali, liked to claim that the Quran gives men permission to beat their women mercilessly, and he's not the first or only person to make that claim. But the Quran I read said something different. It said that you may never strike your wife with anything more substantial than a feather.

Muhammad Ali claimed that his God ordered men to

their deaths in holy wars. But the God I read about declared that suicide is a sin.

As I read on my own, I realized that so much of what I had come to believe about Islam were interpretations made by angry and flawed men. Now that I was immersed in the book itself, I found a text dedicated not to war and vengeance but to peace, mercy, and self-discipline. At first, Muhammad Ali had been happy to see me studying the Quran. His favorite pastime was to sit and play the eminent mufti for hours, holding forth on his great wisdom about the doctrine of Islam. When I'd question or contradict him, he'd quickly grow frustrated, enraged, while I managed to keep my cool, calmly citing the verses that were now my constant companions. He definitely wasn't used to anyone challenging him. Especially not someone who was correct.

Which I was.

"It is compulsory to do jihad!" he told me one day as a rationale for his actions as a terrorist. The Muslims, he said, had to stand up and fight the oppressors, the Quran demanded it.

By this time I'd read the Quran cover to cover, looking for this justification. After he said this, I began to search again for this reference. What I'd found was something very different. So when Muhammad Ali came back again to visit me, I said, "Tell me something. When they used to put Muslim women in the desert and lash the Muslims and starve them, why didn't the Muslims fight back? Why didn't they do jihad?"

"Those were pre-Medina times. At that time, persecution was jihad."

"So what am I doing right now?"

"You're a prisoner."

"I am doing jihad against persecution. And what are you doing?"

"I'm doing jihad against persecution," Muhammad Ali said.

"No, I am a Muslim and you are persecuting me. My jihad is against you. Your jihad is against yourself as well. You would send a suicide truck to blow people up, which results in a retaliatory drone strike, which means your women and children are being killed and villages are being destroyed. That's your idea of jihad. When the Prophet Muhammad did jihad in Medina, he did it to prove how pure he was. Whatever his persecutors did to him, he said only, 'I forgive you in the name of Allah.' This is the jihad the Quran is talking about. The Prophet said, 'When you are being attacked, be steadfast. Hold your ground. Help is on its way.'"

This infuriated Muhammad Ali. He knew only one way to live, the way of violence. A murderous man, he needed a rationale for his twisted instincts, and he had found it in his warped reading of the scriptures. He was a man of God, I will give him that. But it was a God of his own invention. One that existed solely to justify the evil acts he was compelled to commit. He couldn't accept that I found a God in my Quran who gave hope to people who were suffering and offered compassion to those in captivity. His ridiculous demands had exposed him as a fool. In doing so, Muhammad Ali had inadvertently handed me a great gift: I no longer feared him. He could beat me, but he could no longer scare me. If I was going to die alone in a mud hut, the least I could do was tell him that he was a failure and a useless human being.

*His throne extends over the heavens and the earth,*
*and He feels no fatigue in guarding and preserving them,*
*for He is the Highest and Most Exalted.*

Muhammad Ali had been so eager to introduce me to his God. But now that we'd met, I realized He was not the God Muhammad Ali spoke about at all. He was my God, and He was to be respected, and feared, but if you feared Him, you need not fear any man.

Not even Muhammad Ali.

Just as I'd predicted, Muhammad Ali's demands were impossible for my family. By February, he was growing increasingly frustrated. It was becoming clear to him that his master plan, the one he liked to boast of, was deeply flawed. It had been six months and I was still in his possession. He'd failed to turn me, his golden goose, into cash. My family had responded to him in the exact way I knew they would: By explaining that they desperately wanted me home and were willing to negotiate, but they did not have that kind of money or the political clout. They might be able to deliver three or maybe four of the men on the list, and a decent amount of ransom. Rather than bargaining, Muhammad Ali took every protestation as proof of their insolence. He refused to budge on any of his demands, assuming they would cave.

He barged into my room one day. "They are not taking me seriously!" he raged.

What could I tell him? His demands were insane.

Six months on, I began to wonder why I was still alive. Surely, his plan had not been to keep me in captivity for over half a year. If he wanted money, he could have lowered his demands and taken a realistic amount. The whole thing made no sense to me.

Clearly, in his mind, he still had some cards to play.

# 16

One cold afternoon as I was reading the Quran, the locks of my jail door started to rattle. This was my sad version of a doorbell, a sound that meant I was about to receive a visitor. I had eaten, having already received my daily ration of food and water. I assumed my visitor was Muhammad Ali. He would typically check in on me once or twice a week, sometimes a little less frequently.

As Muhammad Ali entered the room, I could tell today was not going to feature one of our usual illuminating chats. He was clearly agitated. Evidently, he came with a specific purpose.

I greeted him with a salaam; he nodded, distracted.

In a previous visit, he'd told me how his muscles ached from sitting on the cold floor of my cell, complaining bitterly of aches and pains in both legs.

I smiled at the irony. *Welcome to my world. The same floor that iced up your poor muscles is where I lie every night.*

"Why are you smiling?" he'd asked me, partly irritated, partly curious.

"You say you're cold. Well, I'm also cold! It's February. Can I at least get some socks and a sweater?" We were well into winter, and the nights were bitingly cold.

He gave me that joyless smile of his, an expression I will not forget. "I have brought you here to make you hard, Shahbaz," he replied, in the tone he adopted when he felt he was teaching me a great life lesson. He loved to tell me how I would benefit from this ordeal, how it would make me a better man. He even promised me that when he was paid off and I was returned home, I'd be able to translate my kidnapping into a prominent political career. His grand schemes, he felt, would make me a star, which was just another delusion he had about how much the world beyond our mud walls cared about him or me.

It was incredibly exhausting to talk to a delusional psychopath all the time. In a strange way, I came to look forward to Muhammad Ali's visits, since they broke up the numbing monotony of my solitary imprisonment. Yet our interactions were maddening, mostly because he was unhinged. He was no fool. He was astute, unlike the dim-witted guards he employed. But his conception of the world was completely twisted. His misguided sense of importance was laughable. Constant interaction with someone like that, for weeks and months, is exhausting. To have an individual like that in control of your entire existence is excruciating.

I'd watched Muhammad Ali that day in my room after I'd asked for the sweater and socks and wondered how a human being could look upon another person's pain, even feel a sense of it himself in the form of his own aching muscles, and still be so ruthless, so detached from humanity. I realized this man had no basic instincts of kindness. He was truly evil, like some macabre villain from an action movie. I'd never before encountered anyone like this, except in films, where the villain usually gets his just deserts. It was depressing to think he would be the last person I would meet in my life.

He'd exited after his last visit with a smug smile, one that said he was doing this to teach me a lesson. Ironically, when he returned now, he was limping and complaining of the cold.

I said, "Salaam," as I usually did, then asked him how his leg was.

He leaned against the wall and stared at me for a long time. Long enough to make me feel uncomfortable.

Finally he said, "Forget how I am. Tell me, what I should do with you?"

"Let me go?" I muttered under my breath. My dark humor was my only remaining tether to sanity.

"Your family doesn't take me seriously. They think I won't kill you."

Trying to reassure him this wasn't true, I replied, "I thought the negotiations were going well." Still assuming he was interested in finding some compromise.

"Not well enough."

He walked toward me and grabbed me by the neck, pressing his thumb into my windpipe. I started to choke.

He shouted in my face, "If I don't get my money and my brothers back, then what use are you to me?"

"I thought things were going well," I breathlessly replied, struggling to free my neck from his grasp. "You told me I would be home soon."

In a violent frenzy he slapped me across my face, threw me to the ground, and kicked me. "This is not a joke!" he yelled.

I wondered who he thought was telling jokes.

Reaching into his pocket, he pulled out an old Nokia cell phone and showed me a homemade video of my mother's car driving near my home in Lahore. "You need to understand I can get your family at any time. When I tell you to do something, you do it." He grabbed me by the hair and lifted my head. "Tomorrow morning I will take you to talk to your mother. Call her, abuse her, remind her that you are running out of time. If you can't convince her, I will kill you right there and then.

"Think long and hard about what you will say tomorrow," he said, standing over me. I curled up, shielding myself. "Your fate is in your hands. If my demands aren't fulfilled tomorrow, I will display your dead body in the Mir Ali bazaar so the whole of Pakistan can see what we can do."

With that, he left the room.

I was petrified that this man who held the balance of my life in his hands was threatening to string me up in the town bazaar. I knew this was a classic Muhammad Ali tactic: There was no way he would simply fetch me for the phone call with no warning. No, he had to tell me a day in advance, beat me, inform me my whole life now hung on what I would say, then give me a day to sit alone to think about what exactly that would entail.

How does one prepare for such a conversation? What does one say? If a deal couldn't be brokered in six months, how on earth could it be settled in a phone call? Not to mention that I was finally being handed an opportunity to talk to my family, whom I had not spoken to in half a year. And the purpose of the conversation was to say goodbye.

I knew I had to choose my words carefully.

At first, I felt emotional and broke down. I didn't want to die. No one does. I prayed to Allah for mercy. I recited *nafal* after *nafal*, verse after verse, prayer after prayer. I read the Quran and did my *dhikr*, a form of rhythmic, repetitive meditation. I asked Allah to forgive me. Would He forgive me? What had I done to deserve this? Perhaps I'd not lived up to my best ideals or led the most righteous life, but what had I ever visited on another human being that meant I deserved to die? Beheaded or worse, in the middle of the wilderness at the hands of madmen.

I knew stronger men than I had faced similar trials and transcended them.

My father spoke often of Nelson Mandela, whom he considered a personal hero. Mandela had spent twenty-seven years in jail by choice for a cause that he believed in. If anyone mentioned my father's imprisonment, my father would always refer to Mandela's great sacrifice.

So what did I believe in?

My father stood in the face of certain death and said he would not give up, even if he was the last man standing.

What was I standing for?

At times these questions threatened to crush me. But in a quiet moment alone I found they started to give me renewed strength. I was no Mandela, I knew that.

But I was Shahbaz Taseer.

If my battle was not political, then I would let it be personal. If I could not change my fate, then I would challenge myself to meet my fate with dignity. I might not be imprisoned for what I believed in, but my captivity could still help me prove to myself what kind of wood I was made of.

I decided in the solitude of my cell that if I was to go, I'd go with courage and self-respect. I would not beg. I would say goodbye to my mother and meet my maker with my head held high, not in arrogance, but out of respect. "I fear no man, for

I only fear you," I would say to my Creator. "I begged from no man for I only ask from you."

It's strange how strong you can stand in the face of adversity when you feel that God stands with you. I believed with all my heart that He was on my side.

Regardless of the outcome of my conversation with my mother, whatever was to happen to me was predestined and, I firmly believed, would be the best outcome for me. If God was calling me home through death, then to Him I would go.

I prepared myself. I said goodbye mentally to all my family and friends.

Lastly, I spoke to my father.

I told him that I loved him and I missed him. Thinking of him had always made me cry, but this last time I was overwhelmed with wonder. I thought, *I am truly going to be with him soon and he will take care of me.*

It may have sounded childish, but it was my last goodbye.

**The door rattled, my strange doorbell. The guard came in** and uncuffed the chains from my arms and legs. He slipped a hood over my head and led me out into the compound. For the first time in months, I felt the touch of outside air on my skin, the warmth of the sun on my body. He hurled me into a car and pushed my face toward the floor.

Off we went.

We drove for about fifteen minutes before arriving at a new compound. The driver parked the car and I was pulled out of the back seat and quickly rushed inside. The guard stripped off my hood, and I saw Muhammad Ali, sitting on the floor with another man, a South Korean who called himself Abdul Ghani. I later found out he had been tasked with translating the negotiations with my mother. Again I said salaam to Muhammad Ali. He angrily ordered my guard to sit me down and make me face the wall. All the while, Muhammad Ali hurled insults at me. He'd succumbed in frustration to a rage. At times when he spoke to me alone in my cell, he could seem reasonable, even thoughtful. But when he lost his temper, he was unhinged, a ranting madman, a lunatic.

He shouted at me, "Your neck is soft. It will be easy to slice through. I will cut it from back to front so you suffer until the moment you die!"

I was sweating, facing the wall. I thought of how as a little kid I'd loved dressing up as Batman for Halloween, and how this was the moment in the story when a superhero would tear through his ropes, turn on his attackers, thrash them thoroughly, then dash to safety. But I was no superhero. And this was real life. This was my life. In its final moments.

Knowing that you are about to be butchered and mutilated for the whole world to see is not how anyone wants to die. It's certainly not how I wanted to go. My father had been taken from me by violence. Did my wife need to be widowed too? Just like my mother?

It seemed certain that my fate was sealed. I tried to recall the calm I had felt back in my room, imagining my reunion with my father. The memory of my father had comforted me, and now I had to lend that same comfort to the people who were going to be tormented by the sight of my death. I could not save myself, but I could be strong for them. I had to be. They would at least know I died with honor and dignity. I prayed that this would make it easier for them, that it would salve their pain in some small way. That they would be proud of me. It's always easier to celebrate bravery than live with cowardice. I had to display courage in these last moments. It was the one last gift I could give them.

Abdul Ghani placed the call. Then Muhammad Ali held the phone to my ear.

# 17

"Shahbaz?"

For the first time in six months, I heard my mother's voice.

She said my name again. I couldn't believe it. It was as though my continuous prayers had finally been answered.

I wanted to cry. I stayed composed.

I said goodbye.

She calmly said, "Don't say goodbye to me!"

We spoke. It was as if I were dreaming.

My mother then handed the phone to my wife and I said, "I am strong and not afraid. I pray five times a day and I know God is merciful. I will be with Abba and we will wait for you."

"Don't say goodbye, Shahbaz. Stay strong."

There's a famous song by Jeff Buckley that I'd always loved, and the lyrics came to me in that dark room:

*This is our last goodbye*
*I hate to feel the love between us die*

*But it's over*
*Just hear this and then I'll go.*

Oddly, the words gave me strength. I knew there was dignity in accepting my fate, and that comfort was the last gift I could give to my family.

So I said the only thing that made sense to me. The same words my father had written to his young wife when they'd been separated against their will. The only words that I thought might offer solace to my family:

"I am not made of a wood that burns easily."

I asked to speak with my mother.

It was good to hear her voice.

I told her that I was proud to be her son and my father's son. I apologized for the pain that she had to suffer because of me. I told her not to watch any videos of my death that my captors might send.

My mother was a lot sterner with me than my wife had been. "Do not talk like that to me ever again!" Firmly she said, "No one will touch you! Do you hear me?" I remember thinking, *What a deluded woman.* Not because she was trying to comfort me. I loved her more than anything else and would have traded the world in that moment to return to my family. But I knew that my mother could not see the place I was in, the men I was with, the circumstances of my captivity. She still lived in a world of civility and compassion. She could not possibly understand the barbarity of my captors or the depth of my deprivation. Her insistence that all this might still end well, that we would figure out a solution as though it were all just a big misunderstanding, seemed laughably absurd. The difference between her and me was that despite the circumstances she still held on to hope. I could hear a mother's protective ferocity boiling up inside her, the urge to protect her child and strike down anyone who might threaten me.

My eyes filled with tears. It was unbelievable to hear their voices. I had been starved of them and they nourished me, just a little bit. They also humbled me. I wanted to tell them how much I loved them, how incomplete my life was without them. But I didn't want to crumble, to beg, to cry out. I could feel my strength wavering. So I simply said I loved them and that it was time for me to say goodbye.

As he listened to our conversation, Muhammad Ali exploded with rage. This was not what he expected at all.

The interpreter took back the phone and began translating Muhammad Ali's threats to my mother. "We will kill him! Just tell us where to send the body!"

My mother knew the authorities had three of Muhammad Ali's coconspirators in custody and said, "If you kill my son, this is over. Don't send me the body. You will get nothing. Do you understand? You will get nothing. I can repeat myself to make it clear. It will be body for body and blood for blood."

When the translator relayed her answer to Muhammad Ali, he became irate. He'd expected me to be on my knees, blubbering, begging for my life, yet I was calmly saying my goodbyes. He'd expected my mother to collapse and concede to his outrageous demands, and she was telling him that if he killed me, he should understand the same fate would fall on three of his own.

They put me back on the phone. I tried to reason with my mother, but she refused to hear me. "Nothing will happen to you. We will bring you home. Tell them to listen to me! I don't have four billion rupees. Tell them to take me instead of you. Tell them to understand that I'm a mother."

That's when it struck me. My mother was in so much pain of her own. She was a widow, her husband violently taken from her just over a year earlier. She had already seen so much anguish, and now she was fighting in vain for me.

"I love you guys so much," I said after a moment of silence. "Keep a good memory of me. I too am made from the same wood as my father."

I disconnected the call.

Muhammad Ali was furious.

For all the power he had over me, for all the ways in which my life was held hostage to his capricious whims, in this moment I could clearly see what a pathetic excuse for a man he was. I witnessed my father stare death in the face and carry on. Muhammad Ali's shallow character could not handle my simple phone call with my mother.

He screamed and cursed. Waving his pistol, he struck me. "You're worthless to me! I might as well kill you now!"

He pointed his gun to my head.

At the height of the controversy around Asia Bibi, as mullahs across Pakistan called for my father's death, I remember asking my father one day if he was scared. He showed me the inscription of the Ayat al-Kursi that hung around his neck and said, "This will protect me." My father strongly believed in the power of prayer. He believed that if you stay true to your convictions, no one on earth can harm you. That was before his own bodyguard killed him in broad daylight. I pondered endlessly during the mourning period whether he'd been wrong to put so much trust in the notion that he couldn't be harmed. But as I sat alone in my cell, I'd come to another understanding of his words. When he said that no one on earth could harm you, he meant people could not take your conviction away. That if you stay true to your beliefs, every attack on you, even one that ends your life, would ultimately be a failure.

I remembered those words as Muhammad Ali pressed the gun barrel against my skull. "Anything else you would like to say before I kill you?"

My father often quoted T. B. Macaulay:

> And how can man die better
> Than facing fearful odds
> For the ashes of his fathers
> And the temples of his Gods.

*Let those be my last words*, I thought, even if only to myself. I shut my eyes and prepared for what was to come.

Then Muhammad Ali pulled the trigger.

**I wish I could tell you I knelt resolutely and faced down** death with stoic grace. I had grown stronger in my time in captivity, but I certainly wasn't that strong, not yet. Not strong enough to release all fear of death, all terror at the notion of saying goodbye to this life.

Making it back home seemed impossible other than through divine intervention. As depleted and pointless as my life had become, I still wanted to live. I still wanted to see my family. Only a miracle could reunite me with the beautiful world I had once belonged to.

Click.

Muhammad Ali laughed perversely.

A callous laugh, the crippled laugh of a person whose only source of joy in this world comes from inflicting misery on others.

The magazine was empty.

He was playing his usual sick mind games.

A panic attack set in and my heart raced. I collapsed to the ground.

"I just wanted to see your reaction," he said.

As the guards hoisted me back up to my feet, I could barely stand. I remember feeling three things. First, I despised Muhammad Ali with a renewed vigor. Second and most important, I was grateful to be alive. Perhaps the angels had protected me after all, just as my father had said.

And finally, despite everything, I felt proud that I'd said goodbye to my family on my own terms.

Muhammad Ali leaned in close to my face as the guards stood me up. As furious as he was, I sensed a grudging respect that I'd managed to say goodbye with such composure.

Now he would put an end to that.

"There will be no bravery in your death," he said in a low whisper. "I will take you apart piece by piece."

If his rantings and my pleadings could not pry his ransom from my family, he'd move on to his next brilliant scheme.

He would torture me. And send videos of it to my family.

I could tell he took pleasure from the prospect of brutalizing me.

I knew that the horrors of my story had taken a sadistic turn toward the unimaginable.

# 18

In late April 2012, I'd been in captivity for eight months. After calling my mother again, Muhammad Ali came to my cell to brief me. He had given my mother seven days to meet his demands. If she failed to, he would kill me. I sensed it gave him great pleasure to relay this news to me.

On April 25—I remember the date—the seven days had elapsed. He came to me and said, "Tomorrow is when I kill you."

I spent that day thinking over my life, contemplating death. It was clear it was about to end. I wasn't fearful, exactly, or regretful. Mostly, I felt an overwhelming sense of helplessness. It's a strange feeling to open your hand and release your grip on hope, but that's just how it feels when you accept that your death is a certainty.

The next day, as promised, he came to collect me. He led me to the room where he made his phone calls.

Abdul Ghani, the translator, was on the phone with my

mother. He smiled as Muhammad Ali and I entered the room. "The boss has decided not to kill your son just yet."

I was given a temporary new lease on a purposeless existence.

Later I'd learn that this was a common tactic among kidnappers, particularly Muhammad Ali: to set a date, a hard deadline, only to change it at the last minute. The purpose was to break the will of both the captive and the family, by pushing them to the edge of despair. He hoped this would bring total and immediate compliance. When it didn't, it infuriated him.

Muhammad Ali, through Abdul Ghani, had demanded that my mother come to Mir Ali in person to continue the negotiations. Who knows what real intention lay behind this peculiar proposal. Even more insane, my mother had agreed to it in theory. But when she later discovered anomalies in the plan, she declined their offer to visit. Only people with a registered ID card for the area were allowed access. Her arrival there would have exposed her contacts with the ISI and other security agencies. She could not allow Muhammad Ali to feel she had any sort of power or reach. I was relieved to hear she was unable to come. As much as I wanted this whole ordeal to be over, I did not want my mother traveling anywhere close to where I was. It killed me to think she would see me this way, tortured, humiliated, and I definitely did not want her joining me as another prisoner.

She was explaining all of this to Abdul Ghani, who relayed it to an outraged Muhammad Ali. He had spared the life of her child, and all he was getting in return was more refusals, more denial. The months of getting nowhere were starting to affect him. He grabbed the phone and started shouting abuse at my mother, words she could not understand.

He spat a few more choice insults at my mother, then

slammed shut the phone. He was cornered and it was his own fault. He'd committed to killing me, then hadn't, and now he couldn't, at least not right away. He'd been thwarted again and come away with nothing.

The sight of an unhinged Muhammad Ali was something to behold. We see people in our lives who lose their temper, who rant and rave and can become quite frightening. But it's probable none are unhinged psychopaths who've severed off a person's head with their own hands. When Muhammad Ali became erratic, he went to an extremely dark place.

He grabbed his automatic pistol, screaming about how my family had failed me, my mother was playing games with him, lying to him, trying to outsmart him, and how he'd just have to kill me after all. He shouted and cursed, waving the gun, while I cowered in the corner until . . . *bang!*

The gun went off and the deafening shot reverberated in the tiny room.

From the look on Muhammad Ali's face, I could tell he'd fired the gun completely by accident. He looked as surprised as I did, as everyone looked around to see who, if anyone, had been shot.

I felt a searing pain in my leg and had the horrible realization that it was me.

Muhammad Ali dropped the gun and rushed over to inspect the wound in my calf, which was gushing blood. The pain was so intense I almost passed out. Fortunately, the bullet had not hit bone, but instead passed through my flesh. He tried to stop the bleeding with a dirty cloth. Later, his men convinced him to bandage my leg properly once they saw how badly swollen it was.

Paralyzed by shock and fear, I thought I'd hit my lowest

point. I hadn't. Not even close. That was yet to come and I wouldn't have long to wait!

**Using this incident to his advantage, Muhammad Ali sent a** message through Abdul Ghani. This was a warning shot and the next bullet was marked for my head. He had decided he needed new methods of persuasion. The days of deadlines and threats were over.

That's when the torture began.

My kidnappers discussed the torture in depth before it started. They told me about the techniques they'd use to attain theatrical perfection on camera. Muhammad Ali would visit me at night and say, "*Taiyari karo*"—prepare yourself—then leave me overnight so that my heart would writhe in fear until the morning. I couldn't sleep. Instead, I prayed all night, searching for solace.

In the morning, they came for me.

The first time, I was taken to a room and hung by my arms from a loop in the ceiling. My guard Omar Turk held a thick leather lash in his hands. The video camera was set up on a tripod. When Muhammad Ali gave the signal, Omar Turk whipped the lash against my naked back.

The video camera captured it all.

With the first lash, I stiffened and screamed. The pain was unimaginable. It was like nothing I'd ever before felt. The second lash hurt just as badly. The third, the same.

He kept going.

My back was stinging and raw and my skin was cut open and seeping. They then took me back to my room and left me there.

That was the first time.

They sent the video by email to my mother. The next day, they came for the sequel.

I was hung again by my wrists. This time I knew what to expect.

Omar Turk lashed me a hundred times.

There was no respite or escape from the merciless lashing. Eventually, my brain switched off; I may have passed out.

Every time I came to, I could hear the sound of the whip making contact with my back, causing waves of agonizing pain.

They unhooked my hands from the metal loop, applied antibiotic, and took me to my room again.

They sent the video recording to my family.

That was the second time.

A few days later, they collected me again. My back was an open wound of oozing lacerations.

They hung me by my arms from the loop and lashed me endlessly.

The entire time, Muhammad Ali stared with fascination. I realized that, beyond his ideology, beyond his jihad, beyond his self-righteousness, he enjoyed the pain of others. I started to wonder if, for him, torturing was not a means to collect a ransom, but rather that kidnapping people for ransom was an excuse to torture them.

They untied my arms. I fell to the ground.


**For some time after the third lashing, I was left alone. I** returned to my regular routine. Food in the morning, my ration of water, then days of solitude. These days ran together in a haze. There was no hope that it would change and no sense of when it would end. Muhammad Ali claimed these torture videos would prompt my family to act, but I knew they'd done all they could. They didn't need some further incentive to bring me home. The unrealistic demands were impossible to meet.

The weather warmed up again on its way toward the stifling blaze of summer. In my room, I could only dream of home.

I'm surrounded by family sitting in the sun-drenched courtyard in the middle of my parents' home. I'm there with my wife, brother, sister, mother, and friends. We tease each other affectionately, and I'm the worst of all, ridiculing my friend Harris or unleashing on my friend Ahsan. This is how we express our affection. Pick out friends and roast them one by one. Shabby T, the master of ceremonies, is at the center of it, quick to laugh and usually the one who gets in the last jab.

I opened my eyes.

Still here.

All this time I was unaware my family was working tirelessly, leaving no stone unturned.

My mother was dealing with Muhammad Ali and his band of mercenaries, trying to negotiate my release; she was also reaching out to local contacts for any information. Government agencies felt the right emissary, someone Muhammad Ali would respect, could help broker a deal much more successfully.

When the time came to meet the emissary, Muhammad Ali, ever suspicious, paranoid, sent a low-level functionary to meet with the point man. One unfortunate tendency of his was to surround himself with people of low IQ. Many of his lackeys were barely smart enough to get dressed in the morning, let alone hold high-level negotiations for a hostage release. Sure enough, when Muhammad Ali's man in Mir Ali met with the emissary, the lackey was dismissive and disrespectful, accusing the emissary of being an ISI spy. The lackey reported back that he suspected the whole thing had been a setup orchestrated by the ISI to flush the kidnappers out. Muhammad Ali sent an enraged email to my mother, cursing her and telling her she would get nowhere with these "ISI maulvies."

This outburst did not sit well with Haji Khalil ur Rehman Haqqani, a high-ranking Taliban leader and ally to the Haqqani network. They held a follow-up meeting with Muhammad Ali's head of intelligence, who brought a recorder with him to record the negotiations. Haji told him to turn off the recorder.

"What is this email you wrote to that woman?" Haji asked, meaning the one sent to my mother.

Muhammad Ali's point man got nervous and tried to argue that he was just a middleman, and that the IMU wasn't even responsible for kidnapping me, they were just negotiating on behalf of the real kidnappers.

Haji interrupted, "We know everything. I know who has him, I know how much you're asking for ransom, I know everything about every commander in this territory. We are the Taliban. We *made* these groups. They only exist because we allow it. Now you want to write that we're ISI maulvies?"

The lackey was petrified.

"You ever write anything like that again," Haji said, "you'll have a bigger problem than this boy."

When the lackey reported this conversation back to Muhammad Ali, he was visibly shaken. I'd never seen him in such a state before. He knew that, for all the power he had in his own little group, he depended on the good graces of the Taliban and their allies to continue to exist in this territory. He had a fragile ego and was not used to cowering down to authority. This was the first time I'd seen fear in his eyes.

I savored it.

I'd been snatched by Uzbek extremists who were repressive and brutal, unlike the Taliban, who somewhat followed a code of conduct. The Taliban kidnapped for ransom, and the captive was often treated as well as or better than the kidnappers themselves. Captives were fed, clothed, and held without torture. What's more, the Afghan Taliban leadership could be reasoned with. They saw themselves as representing the interests of the people of Afghanistan. While the group was regarded as little better than terrorists in the Western world, in the tribal regions they were celebrated as freedom fighters. The government of Pakistan had long had official or semiofficial diplomatic relationships with them to maintain a tenuous peace.

These Uzbek terrorists were wild cards. They seemed to have no permanent loyalty to any group and no goals beyond unending violence. My mother's emissary returned from the meeting frustrated and insulted. He relayed that, despite the setbacks, he believed he could negotiate a deal if my family could secure the release of Mumtaz Qadri and maybe two or three others from the list of detainees, along with a sizable ransom. "Give me two or three men from the list, it doesn't even matter who."

My mother held a sad meeting with my two siblings, explaining to them that the release of Qadri, our father's murderer, could be instrumental in securing my freedom. In Pakistan, if the family of a murdered person forgives the killer, the killer is set free.

Without hesitation they both immediately gave their consent.

Meanwhile, humiliated and frustrated, Muhammad Ali had decided my family were to be tormented.

This meant punishing me.

# 19

It had been several days since my last torture session. Muhammad Ali decided it had not been brutal enough. It was time to up the ante.

He would typically arrive to disclose his plans for the following day, making sure I would stew all night imagining the horrors of tomorrow.

As an uneventful day drew to a close, Muhammad Ali took me from my room into an adjacent chamber and sat me down at a table. A guard, Sohail, sat behind me to hold me still. Muhammad Ali held a special torture tool, a *plass*, pliers. The video camera was already set up. The whole production had a clinical air, almost like a doctor's appointment.

I was given a single painkiller injection in the flesh above each nail. This wasn't to completely numb the pain—there would be plenty of that—but simply to make sure I didn't pass out. This was all to ensure the video had maximum impact. It was to be as gruesome as possible with me in as much agony as the camera could capture. "You have to start screaming as soon as we start and keep screaming until we are done," Muhammad Ali commanded, like a film director. "The louder you scream, the sooner this will be over." It was surreal to sit there receiving these instructions as though I were their accomplice, not their victim.

Muhammad Ali injected the painkiller into my fingers, then spread my hand on the table.

He took the nail of my thumb in his pliers and started to pry it loose.

At first there was only pain. The agony was so intense I came close to vomiting. But the nail wouldn't come loose, which meant the action was useless for his torture video. So they stopped the recording and Muhammad Ali took a small blade and cut across the top of the nail on each finger, to loosen it. Then they started the video again.

This time, he decided to skip the thumb. With the pliers, he ripped off the fingernail of each finger on my right hand. With each yank a white-hot pulse of pain throbbed through my entire body. My hand on the table was covered in blood. He took my nails and placed them in a small plastic bag. A messenger would soon be arriving. He'd have these nails sent to my mother in Lahore.

**When it was all over, I was crying and delirious with pain.** The guard swabbed my naked nail beds in Pyodine, which hurt almost as much as having the nails pulled off. Slowly the pain began to ebb. My fingers were bandaged, the camera switched off; the show over, they took me back to my room.

I had been reduced to the lowest form of life you could find on earth. The pain was one aspect, it was excruciating. Beyond my pain and degradation what almost defeated me was what a burden my family would also bear. These videos, the gruesome evidence of my lowest moments, would be delivered to them. Rendered helpless, I felt the humiliation threatened to swallow me whole.

Another night, not long after, Muhammad Ali came to my room. "Ahmed," he said, using one of the code names they used to keep my identity secret, "tomorrow we cut flesh from your back."

I was quite aware of the horrendous agony that would ensue for days.

The next day they took me back to the torture cell. My shirt was removed; I was made to stand in a large plastic bin and tied by the wrists to the loop in the ceiling.

I realized the purpose of the plastic bin was to catch all the blood that would stream from my body.

Muhammad Ali stood behind me, a sharp knife in his hand. He drew the knife down my skin, cutting a long strip of flesh from my back.

The pain was indescribable. I screamed and screamed. But again, the pain was not the worst of it.

I was consumed by an overwhelming sense of disbelief that my life had ended up here. In the hands of these madmen, desecrating me. The sense of desperation at my situation, the suffocating conviction that somehow I deserved all of this, took me to a dark place.

Muhammad Ali cut a second strip of flesh from my back, a few inches long.

He held it up to my face for me to see.

Did I pass out? I may have. It's hard for me to recount the individual moments of my torture. They were a series of sensations, sounds, moments, all played out against a backdrop of searing pain.

They cleaned me up and applied antibiotic. Then bandaged the worst of my cuts.

I was returned to my hovel, where I collapsed, unsure whether it was day or night, summer or winter, or if I was dead or alive.

**My family received six videos over three weeks. A** schedule emerged. One day of torture, two days to recover. I had no idea how the videos were being received or who was watching them. My life was reduced to being tortured, recovering from being tortured, and waiting to be tortured again.

The pain and humiliation remained constant.

**Now, finally, it was time to make another phone call.**

We didn't call from the compound. Muhammad Ali had grown too paranoid, full of conspiracy theories. He believed the ISI or the CIA would triangulate on his cell phone and launch a drone strike against us.

I wished they would.

If I could only see the look on his face as a missile approached, right before blowing us all sky-high, it would make it worthwhile for me.

Omar Turk yanked me to my feet and dressed me in a burka. I recalled the first days of my captivity when I was in the ketamine haze being dragged from town to town. It seemed like a million years ago, as if it happened to a different person. That version of Shahbaz had felt the cosseting touch of his car's luxurious leather interior only hours before. He was a citizen of a different world.

This Shahbaz, the one in the room, the one the guards only called Jee Bhai, or Ahmed, had only visited that world in fragments of half-remembered dreams.

They escorted me outside. After so many days and weeks in the dark indoors, I stumbled as I squinted against the bright sun.

Shoved into the back seat of a nondescript car, I was told we were going to the Mir Ali bazaar.

**The world looked strange.**

We drove along a dusty road past low-slung, single-story mud buildings. Farmers stared as we passed. Self-styled mujahideen stood on the road in *shalwar kameez*. Not many people were around, but to me, after so many months with the same handful of guards and under the watch of one madman, it was alien to see people at all. I wondered what would happen if I cried out, "I'm Shahbaz Taseer, help me," if I tried to appeal to their mercy. I'm sure they would have just kept staring. Or most likely looked away. They had seen all manner of horrors in this part of the world. The plight of an undernourished, straggly man wouldn't move them in the least.

We approached a street near the edge of the central market in Mir Ali and parked. I was seated next to the translator, Abdul Ghani. Muhammad Ali turned around and handed me a cell phone. We'd make the call from here, he explained. That way if the call was traced, they would not know where we were.

Abdul Ghani dialed my mother's number and handed me the phone.

The conversation was similar to the first one we'd had:

"Tell them to take me, Shahbaz. Tell them to take me instead."

Just as Muhammad Ali had instructed, I calmly explained to my mother that she needed to meet their demands. She said she could collect a lesser amount and ensure the release of four or five prisoners at best.

Muhammad Ali refused that offer.

Around us, outside the car, life swirled through the Mir Ali market. Women inspected food from farmers' carts and men haggled over goods. Children ran, shouting at one another, playing games. It was all happening just on the other side of the thin glass of the car's windows.

Abdul Ghani ended the call. All those weeks of torture, all the videos, had changed nothing. My family remained unable to persuade Muhammad Ali to show some flexibility.

He sat in the front seat, fuming. He was not used to his requests being denied. He seemed ready to shoot me, his driver, himself, or all of us.

Then a knock came at his window.

We sat, silent.

I couldn't imagine who would dare to bother us. In Mir Ali, clearly everyone knows who the mujahideen are, who the terrorists are, and people know to keep their distance.

Muhammad Ali rolled down his window.

"Water, water," said a boy selling bottled water. He held a plastic bottle up to the open window.

Muhammad Ali, unnerved, stared in terror. "Go! Go!" yelled Muhammad Ali at the driver, who started the car and raced off.

The ISI had found us, Muhammad Ali was sure of it. No regular boy would dare bother a car full of mujahideen. The boy had to be a spy, a scout, sent to pinpoint our location for a drone strike. Muhammad Ali was ranting. The car careened quickly through the narrow lanes of the town, kicking up dust.

Muhammad Ali was paranoid; he'd had spies among his own men before, some of whom he'd executed. As we sped away, he became convinced a motorcycle was following us.

"Go! Faster, faster!" he yelled.

I looked behind us. It was true, a motorcycle was on our tail.

No part of me thought this whole adventure would end in my being whisked to safety or with secret agents coming to my rescue. If these were indeed ISI agents, and I had no reason to believe they were, I'd simply die now in a hail of gunfire, along with this group of mercenaries.

As we sped out of town, we hit a minor sandstorm that whipped up dirt to cover our escape, if indeed there was anything to escape from. Eventually, we lost our tail. Muhammad Ali could not relax. He was agitated about the audaciousness of the water boy. I realized, maybe for the first time, that my extended captivity, the endless weeks of negotiations leading nowhere, the failing tactics and the absence of any plan to go forward, were taking a toll on him.

The next day he announced we were packing up from our headquarters and moving. We'd find a new safe house to stay in.

For a few weeks, we moved from house to house to avoid detection. The kidnappers' network of associates in and around Mir Ali made it simpler to find new hiding spots. Eventually, Muhammad Ali settled on a small house adjacent to the much-larger dwelling occupied by Abu Yahya al-Libi, a high-ranking official in al-Qaeda. The IMU was not officially under the umbrella of al-Qaeda. Technically, the IMU was allied with the Afghan Taliban.

Thus I ended up residing in a small mud room with my new guard, Saleem. It was no different, no better or worse, than the previous rooms I'd stayed in.

Little did I know when I moved into this room that this would be the place where I would allegedly die.

# 20

The *New York Times* described the events that took place in North Waziristan on June 4, 2012:

In the world of violent global jihad, Abu Yahya al-Libi was an evangelist, a philosopher and a social media rock star. He was even being mentioned as a likely candidate to take over as the head of Al Qaeda.

"I call him a man for all seasons for A.Q.," Jarret Brachman, a former analyst for the Central Intelligence Agency (CIA), said in *The Times* in 2008. "He's a warrior. He's a poet. He's a scholar. He's a pundit. He's a military commander. And he's a very charismatic, young, brash rising star within Al Qaeda."

U.S. officials said Tuesday that a drone strike in Pakistan's tribal belt had killed Mr. Libi . . . He was killed early Monday morning in a strike by a Central Intelligence Agency drone in North Waziristan, according to the U.S. officials. On Tuesday, the Pakistani government summoned a senior

American diplomat to the Foreign Ministry to relay its "serious concerns" over continuing drone strikes in the tribal areas.

At the time that this was published I had no way to read *The New York Times*. Then again, I didn't need to. I was there.

Of the 1,657 days that passed during my four and a half years in captivity, June 4, 2012, is one I will never forget. On that day, I was killed as part of a drone strike on one of al-Qaeda's most wanted terrorists. He had escaped from Bagram prison seven years earlier. I was just another piece of collateral damage in the U.S. war on terror.

At least, that was the official story. The one my mother was told. And the one the world came to believe.

Let me recap that fateful day.

**I sat in a dark, dingy mud room, unwashed, shackled, and** talking to Saleem. As far as guards went, he was among the less evil. He'd been my guard before; he had brought me the razor and bowl the first time I'd been allowed to shave. While he watched over me, he didn't beat me, he didn't insult me, and despite hailing from Kazakhstan, he spoke enough Urdu for us to communicate.

Like many of the young men I'd encountered in my year of captivity, Saleem was naive and inexperienced in the ways of this sinister, uncertain world. Many of these men signed on to a holy war with great enthusiasm after promises of untold honor and glory and without much understanding of the demands to be made of them. For Saleem, it meant sitting in a dusty and stiflingly hot mud hut for hours, watching over this shriveled, bearded man he'd come to know as Ahmed. We were barely acquainted.

Muhammad Ali had been shifting me from safe house to safe house for weeks to avoid detection. He had become increasingly frantic and paranoid. The ISI definitely knew that I was somewhere in the vicinity of Mir Ali.

Whether or not they knew my whereabouts, they could do little or nothing to rescue me.

A covert operation would end in certain failure, as in the case of an ambush my captors would immediately dispose of me.

My latest location was a safe house that adjoined the home of Abu Yahya al-Libi, a top al-Qaeda leader. In this part of Pakistan, such a home offered maximum security or the closest thing to it. Not even the greediest of locals would think to sell out such a high-ranking member of al-Qaeda. Al-Libi's home was modest by most standards, just a mud dwelling with a second and third floor, but it stood out in Mir Ali for its relative grandeur. My room was attached to the side of his house like an afterthought.

That fateful day, June 4, as Saleem and I sat aimlessly staring into space, there was a tremendous boom, then blackness. That, I would learn firsthand over the next few years, is how a drone strike works. It was all about surprise. If you're indoors, the drones come with no warning at all. Just the quiet of the day suddenly ended by noise and annihilation. Following the calm after the explosion, there was chaos and destruction. The ceiling caved in, killing Saleem immediately, and a wall collapsed, leaving me bruised and bloodied, but giving me cover from the worst of the blast. In the dust and confusion of the aftermath, I lay unable to move because of my shackles. I was perceived dead.

Men started shouting and searching through the rubble for survivors. In all the chaos, I coughed, then began to choke.

This caught Muhammad Ali's attention, and he looked across and saw me move.

He signaled to his men. "Put that dead body in the car!" They unchained my body, stashed me in the back seat of a car, and drove me away to another safe house. I was starting to realize that, in North Waziristan, *safe house* is a relative term.

The notorious al-Libi had survived the strike and was buried in his basement under the rubble. A few of his men were trying to get him out. That's when a second drone strike hit the house. The second strike killed everyone who was left inside, including Abu Yahya al-Libi. In the fifteen minutes or so between the first strike and the second, I'd been transported to safety. I had been confined in a house packed with terrorists, among whom I was the sole survivor.

If there is such a thing as a miracle, I'd just experienced it.

As I lay in the back seat of the car, I was informed of the second strike. It had destroyed the compound, killing everyone. Multiple injuries were making it difficult for me to breathe, but I was alive.

We drove at high speeds over rutted dirt roads, my body rattling in the back seat. When we pulled up to the designated safe house, a number of guards lifted my limp body and carried me inside, laying me on the floor. That was to be my bed. For now, another mud room would be my hospital.

For the first few days and nights I was delirious, suffering from panic attacks. I had crazed, vivid, overwhelming dreams, full of loud shattering sounds. I'd wake up and lie motionless. No bones were broken, yet I felt battered as though I'd been hit by a bus. Slowly my body started to heal, but it would be weeks before I could sit up and months more before I could walk unaided.

With fall approaching, Muhammad Ali realized he could

no longer shuttle me from safe house to safe house. He'd stashed me in one of the safest places in Mir Ali and almost lost me with nothing to show for it. So in August, he began building a room for me in the compound where he lived. Meanwhile, I was held at the house of a man named Mutavakal, who watched over me during my convalescence. He showed me compassion. When I could stand, he let me take a shower. He stopped my goat-fat diet and fed me food. He was still my captor, but he lacked the streak of cruelty that delighted the men who'd previously guarded me.

When I was moved into a different room, I started to have terrible visions. Were they surreal dreams or an underlying message? Each night, I felt an inescapable fear that I was being descended upon by ghosts. The apparitions were like moving shadows that attacked me. I'd shake all night, screaming and sweating. Despite Mutavakal's kindness, I begged Muhammad Ali to move me somewhere new.

To make matters worse, after a few weeks at this safe house, I caught malaria. The disease was a constant concern in Mir Ali, thanks to its swarms of mosquitoes, whose buzzing sounds still haunt me to this day. The town has no proper sewage system, only open gutters in the streets. Muhammad Ali was, true to his nature, thrilled at the severity of my illness.

To him, malaria was like another form of torture, one that spared him any effort. For the first couple of days, as I lay shivering on the ground, my head throbbing with a burning fever, he refused to give me any medicine. He sat over me, yelling, "Give me the bank accounts! What are the numbers!" He'd convinced himself I was holding out some secret financial information that would unlock the hidden, untold riches that he felt so close to accessing.

I felt as if I'd been poisoned. No different from a slug's

reaction when salt is poured on it. I was now at my wit's end. I told Muhammad Ali in a quavering voice there were no secret bank accounts, no hidden information. I begged him for medicine, which he flatly refused. At first, that I'd survived the drone seemed like a miracle, but now it was a cruel joke. I'd lived through that ordeal only now to die on a mud floor.

When it became clear he was withholding the medicine as a tactic to pry information from me, I simply told him, "Let me die."

**After the drone attack, the ISI determined through local** informants that I had been present at the site of the strike. Given that the house I'd been kept in was now a twice-struck pile of pebbles, with a death count of roughly eighteen people, naturally it was assumed I had been killed.

The general in charge called my mother. His exact words were "Shahbaz Taseer is no more. We have confirmed sources to believe he has been killed in a drone strike."

Refusing to believe this, my mother patiently continued to wait for a call from the kidnappers. In November the general called my mother to say they had new intel on me. There had been a sighting. "He is alive."

My death was widely reported on Pakistani news. "Shahbaz Taseer Killed in Drone Attack: Taliban Sources" was a typical headline that greeted the world.

Muhammad Ali saw the widespread news of my death as an opportunity. He would tell my family that I was dead, despite knowing I was slowly recuperating. His thinking was, if he pushed them to the edge of mourning, he could reveal to them in the coming months that I was still alive, and they'd be so relieved they'd finally cough up his ransom.

So he relayed the news of my death to Mama: "Shahbaz Taseer is dead."

**What I couldn't know, lying there broken in the dark, is that** when the ISI general called my mother to report my death to her, she did not cry or wail. She did not faint or break down. She answered flatly, "Where is the body?" The general tried to explain to her that drone strikes rarely leave identifiable corpses, so casualties are counted based on who was known to be in the residence at the time. "Show me the body," my mother repeated firmly. She had lost her husband and watched them bury him in the ground.

The ISI was unable to produce a body, so she continued to believe I was alive. She kept on hoping. My mother shielded the rest of my family from this unverified report.

**After nearly a week of leaving my malaria untreated,** Muhammad Ali relented and put me on an IV drip of medicine. I think he realized that he could torture me all he liked, but I was no good to him dead. After that, my vitals improved. I began to heal. Though unsure what the future held, I'd survived my first run-in with a drone.

One day Muhammad Ali brought a young man to my room to see me. I recognized him as Ahmed; he had the same name my captors used for me. He was one of the occasional guards who'd been watching over me in my first year. I wasn't sure why he had been produced, but Ahmed looked terrified.

Muhammad Ali explained that he'd learned that Ahmed was a spy, paid by the ISI to relay my location to them. How much of the Ahmed tale was true? It was impossible for me to judge. The intelligence forces certainly relied on, and often got, paid cooperation from impoverished locals. I could definitely believe that they had many such informants in and around Mir Ali. Whatever the truth, Muhammad Ali was taking Ahmed's alleged betrayal seriously. This, Muhammad Ali explained to me, was why he'd been so paranoid in the bazaar when the water-selling boy approached his car! Muhammad Ali also crowed that this proved how valuable I was to the government, how much of an embarrassment my kidnapping had been, and how much they wanted to cover it all up. Once again, Muhammad Ali had found a way to convince himself his hard-line tactics would pay off in the end.

After Ahmed confessed, Muhammad Ali dragged him away. I found out later that that he was taken to the bazaar in the middle of town, had a land mine strapped under his feet, and was blown up. This execution was meant to serve as an example to anyone who took the ISI's money.

Not long after that, my room at Muhammad Ali's compound was completed. Rather than risk any more betrayals, he would keep me with his family. Once I was well enough to be transported, I was moved into his home.

**In Lahore, my case was declared closed. To everyone** outside my family, the story of Shahbaz Taseer was over, another tragic tale in a chaotic country.

Then I was spotted.

Shahbaz Taseer had survived.

My mother would later tell me that she was relieved. The call confirmed to her that her son was still alive, which she had known in her heart to be true all along. She'd held on to her hope against all odds. She would need to hold on to it for quite a bit longer.

Abba and me in 1986.

At the time, I was a DC fan.
Then I discovered Tony Stark.

Taking my very first steps.

My father celebrating an election victory in 1986.

Exploring the ruins of Ephesus in Turkey with my father and brother, my two favorite people.

My mother and me in January 1986, the day we brought my brother, Shehryar, home from the hospital.

My mother and father in Lahore in 2009 with
the then Secretary of State Hillary Clinton.

A family portrait at Shehryar's university
graduation in 2005.

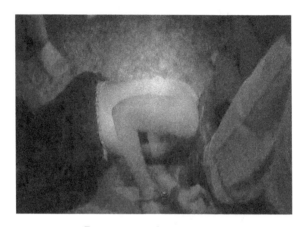

Being tortured in captivity.

The incisions on my back, carved into me
with blades.

I was lashed one hundred times every day
for almost a week.

They buried me up to my neck for hours
at a time for three days.

My first steps toward reuniting with my family in 2016. This one was for the 'Gram.

The first photograph taken with my family in five years.

Presenting a talk at Cornell University in March 2018.

My miracle, Serena Amy Taseer, and me in our Manchester United jerseys.

Speaking at the House of Commons in London in 2018.

Giving a lecture at Columbia University in 2018 that coincided with Malala Yousafzai's return to Pakistan.

Being interviewed in 2017 about the Premier League season and my club, Manchester United.

My appearance on *BBC HARDtalk* with Zeinab Badawi in 2016.

Neha and me just before the birth of our son,
Shavez Ali Taseer. (Alee' Hassan)

# 21

Time stood still. I remained a hostage tethered to a floor, confined to a room with four mud walls. I was weak and recovering from malaria, still bearing the pain of all the injuries I'd suffered in the drone strike, reeling from the endless hours of torture. Shackled during the day, I had only the floor to sleep on. The bitter cold ruthlessly cut through my battered body, amplifying my misery. My existence was entirely at my captors' mercy. I continued receiving my meager daily rations of food and water. Life was a mirror image of before. But the new site of my captivity was very different from the previous ones in one important aspect.

It was a home.

This was Muhammad Ali's home, the last place on earth I wanted to be a captive, let alone a guest. Bizarrely it seemed like an upgrade.

The dwelling was rudimentary, a single-story structure made of mud walls and a dirt floor, with straw mats on the floor and modest wooden furniture. The main house consisted of two large rooms, one for Muhammad Ali and his wife, and one for the matriarch of the house, Aya Jaan, Muhammad Ali's mother-in-law and the widow of Muhammad Tahir Farouk, the founder of the IMU. Unlike the squalid barracks I'd stayed at earlier, this compound had women in it and was well-kept, clean, and organized. There were children, too, ranging in age from toddlers to teenagers. I had not been around women or children in a long time.

The home had a different energy, different smells, different sounds. I could hear children playing beyond my door. Above the floor of my room, a small section of the wall had been carved out for air circulation. This opening, a few feet in height and about a foot wide and covered with wire mesh, looked out into a central courtyard. Muhammad Ali had hung a black fabric across the courtyard to cordon off the area reserved for the women. I could often hear their voices, and their laughter, making me realize I hadn't heard laughter in over a year.

Thanks to these small changes, and humble doses of humanity, I felt less dehumanized.

**The women of the household, including Aya Jaan and the** teenaged brides of Muhammad Ali's soldiers, kept themselves concealed and never interacted with me. Some of the older boys were already hardening into the cruel men I knew they would inevitably become. It was almost impossible to be raised in such a backward culture of violence and not lose yourself.

But there was one exception.

Muhammad Ali had a teenaged brother-in-law named Abdul Aziz. From the moment I met him, he treated me fairly. He did not free me or hatch a plan to get me home, but he showed me respect and kindness, which had come to seem like an unimaginable luxury. At first, there was a language barrier between us. He conversed in Pashto and Uzbek but not Urdu or English. Within a month of my arrival, we'd picked up enough of each other's languages to be able to understand one another. He was the first person I'd interacted with in over a year. A simple kind gesture would leave me emotional.

Abdul Aziz came into my room one day and saw me shivering. He asked if I was unwell.

"I'm sleeping on the floor and it is freezing." When I'd wake up, my muscles would be so painfully cramped I could barely move. None of this was new to me; it had been my reality for a year. I told him because he had asked. I never thought he'd do anything to help.

The next day, he came back to my room with a *chatai*, a thin mattress made of straw and horsehair. He also brought me a blanket. He told me he'd spoken to his mother, Aya Jaan, who had voiced her concern about my well-being. Abdul Aziz was aware of the torture, and I could tell that it upset him. But he was not in a position to speak up or ask Muhammad Ali to stop.

I now had a mattress to sleep on and a blanket to keep me warm. I thought back to my first night sleeping chained to the floor, huddled next to the red bucket. I had taken basics, such as a warm, comfortable bed, for granted my whole life. This kindness from Abdul Aziz overwhelmed me.

The following day Abdul Aziz asked if I had slept well. I was much more comfortable, I told him, but because my back was still healing from all the lashings I had endured, the straw of the mattress irritated the wounds. Again, I didn't expect him to do anything about this as it had been so long since anyone had expressed any concern for me.

He nodded.

Later that day, he returned with a sheet.

This was astounding. Here was someone actually listening to my woes, trying to do something to make me more comfortable. I wanted to weep with gratitude.

The biggest gift, however, came a few days later, a small package bearing a few items, the kinds of things I had not held in my hands for over a year. He brought me a small bottle of shampoo and a towel for use after a shower. The towel, actually a bath mat, I accepted gratefully. In all my time at the various safe houses over the previous year, I'd taken only a few showers. Muhammad Ali's home had a small bathroom off my room, where Abdul Aziz allowed me to shower every three days or so. It wasn't an actual shower, just a room with space to wash yourself, but I was given hot water and privacy, which were rare gifts.

Abdul Aziz also brought me a fresh cake of soap, packed in a cardboard box with a suggestive picture of a voluptuous woman. As he handed it over, I glanced at the picture and smirked at him. I had not seen a photo of a woman in over a year. To me, this cardboard box might as well have been a *Playboy* magazine.

I thought he'd find it funny. Instead, he got flustered and grabbed the box back from me. "No, no, no," he kept saying, as though worried he'd get in trouble. Red with embarrassment, he tore up the box. I didn't mind. Soap Box Lady could live on in my dreams, at least for a little while.

———

### The most pleasant change was the children.

They brought joy into my otherwise dark and sad life, which had been bereft of happiness for too long.

Muhammad Ali was a father of seven including Muhammad Tahir, an orphan born to a soldier who'd been killed, an infant not even a year old when I arrived. These kids—Fatimah, almost three; Zakia, a shy five-year-old; six-year-old Fateh; eight-year-old Muhammad; and Omar and Jaffer, who were nine and ten—would from time to time come in to visit me. I was this stranger in their house with the peculiar jewelry around his wrists. Always happy to see them, I treated them with great affection, inquiring about their days and activities and mostly playing games they liked. These innocent children were blameless and had no idea that I was a prisoner, not a guest. Interaction with them brought a softness to my day and began to heal my lonely heart. Out of respect the younger children called me Babuji, a courteous form of *uncle*. After a year of being called Ahmed or Jee Bhai, both names of derision, Babuji fell on my ears like a soothing balm.

Being confined to my room all day, I'd been tasked by Muhammad Ali with teaching the children to speak Urdu. A guard would come in, unchain me, and then my students would arrive for their lesson. We'd sit cross-legged and I'd instruct them in simple words, and they picked up the language faster than I expected.

At the end of each session, it saddened me that these children would never know a normal childhood. I often heard their mother berating them angrily, screaming and violently striking them without restraint. With little notice the house would suddenly fill up with the sounds of an angry man screaming at his wife, who could not protest, prompting her to expel her frustration and anger on the children. Once Fatimah, the three-year-old, was beaten so badly by her mother her face was black-and-blue and her eyes were swollen shut.

Disturbingly, these children were born into and lived every day in a culture of violence and war, which appeared to be their norm. They'd live their lives in war, and war would eventually consume them. It was inevitable. For their parents, education was taboo. The children were forbidden to read any books besides the Quran and were only told stories of the glories of violent jihad. There was no TV; all of that was *haram*, forbidden. They had no traditions of folklore or fairy tales.

This was driven home to me one day when I was playing with Fatimah. A beautiful little girl with bright eyes and a smile that lit up the room, she enjoyed our time together, and I always treated her with great affection and care.

Fatimah loved to draw and brought in a few pieces of paper and some pencils so we could sketch together.

She sat down and asked me to draw her a truck, just like her father's.

I drew one to make her happy. Then, with a flourish, I added a flower sticking out of the back of the truck.

Her little face contorted with anger. "Why did you draw that?" she demanded.

"Because it's a pretty flower."

"But I have to carry out a suicide bombing," she said angrily. "No one will think I'm serious with a flower on my truck."

I nearly cried at her words.

In first few months in this compound with these children, I realized their indoctrination started when they were very young. It came to represent an inexplicable contradiction to me. I'd seen firsthand how protective Muhammad Ali could be about his children, how quickly he'd rush to shield them. Despite all his aggression and viciousness toward me, he was a doting father. Yet here was his three-year-old daughter, who should have been in school singing nursery rhymes, lecturing me about the logistical consistencies of a suicide bombing. Engulfed by sadness, in my protective nature I wanted to spirit her away, but all I could do was save a thought for her in my daily prayers and hope she'd find her way to the security of a happy life.

**At night, as I lay on the straw mattress, gazing out my win-**dow with my face resting on the ground, I had a different perspective. Above the black curtain that Muhammad Ali had hung in the courtyard, I could see the top of a tree.

The next time Abdul Aziz came to visit me, I asked him what it was.

"It's an *anaar* tree," he said. A pomegranate tree. It had been planted a while ago, but it hadn't yet given fruit.

I knew those trees well. We had several in our garden at our farm in Lahore.

In the evening or the morning, when there was enough light to see it, I'd gaze out at that tree. I could only see a few branches peeking up over the black sheet, but after spending a year in mud rooms with no windows, at times I felt that the pomegranate tree, yearning for the sky, was the most beautiful thing I'd seen in my life.

# 22

In the aftermath of the drone strike Muhammad Ali had to lie low, which meant spending more time in this sanctuary of his, at best described as a rudimentary home. However, his visits to me were increasingly infrequent.

His brilliant master plan had gone horribly wrong. I now had a CinemaScope view of him and was privy to the actual person behind the persona. Certainly he wasn't the ferocious mujahideen he portrayed himself to be, but a fairly simple-minded average family man.

The same man who had tortured me, humiliated me, cursed my name, and insulted my family, I now saw interacting with his children, sitting patiently with them on his lap, telling them stories or wiping their tears when they cried.

If I thought any of this apparent softness had taken the edge off his psychotic taste for torture, I was mistaken. He was now out of options with me. His only recourse was to kill me or think of more elaborate ways to torment me physically, in the hope that one of the gruesome videos would finally break my family. He genuinely seemed to enjoy torturing. I know his deputies did.

My main guard at this time was Abdul Momin, a little man reminiscent of a poisoned dwarf, who proudly boasted of having beheaded two prostitutes, a sickening story he would narrate at any opportunity. To him it was his life's greatest achievement.

If Fatimah was a ray of sunshine, he tipped the scales as a vile, puny, and insignificant man both physically and spiritually, with a scraggly beard, unkempt appearance, and unremarkable squat face.

Of all the characters in this dark episode, Abdul Momin stood out as possibly the most detestable.

He looked at me as though I were subhuman, nothing. I'd never been looked at by anyone that way. Not before and not since. Not even Muhammad Ali, in all his cruelty, had that kind of contempt for me. It was infuriating. I'm sure Abdul Momin hated me. I felt the same way.

To pass the time and amuse himself, he would sit and hurl abuse at my mother and my family. He would use every insult under the sun. I didn't care at all about what he thought, but it's wearying to be barraged for hours on end with no hope of relief or escape. I was no longer the Jee Bhai of all those months in the previous safe house, the broken man who'd come to believe he deserved all the scorn these idiots heaped upon him. Now I was Babuji! Being around the children had rekindled my spirit, for better or worse, and I had reached a breaking point.

I devised a strategy for Muhammad Ali's next visit to cunningly appeal to his fragile ego. My strategy was to remind him not to allow Abdul Momin to derail his otherwise brilliant plan. Muhammad Ali should deal with me. Not this guard. I was *his* prisoner. He came up with the master plan. I knew enough that I should not try to appeal to his mercy. I played to the notion that he alone should have dominion over me, not some lackey. This crazy tactic worked. Muhammad Ali took Abdul Momin off the detail and put another guard on me.

The replacement for the poisonous toad Abdul Momin was Sohail, a stark contrast. He'd been around for a while, but now he would be my primary keeper. He was not kind by any stretch, or even decent; however, compared to Abdul Momin, Sohail did not barrage me with insults. He spoke English and was interested in learning Urdu, and sometimes he acted as an intermediary between Abdul Aziz and me.

For me, this changing of the guard represented a great improvement. Little could I have guessed that my switch to Sohail would also bring about a tiny miracle that in all likelihood restored my sanity.

One uneventful day, while sitting around, he tepidly, casually asked a simple but life-changing question:

"Brother, are you fond of sports?"

I couldn't believe my ears.

**My maternal grandfather had been a semiprofessional** cricket player. My father was mad about sports. Cricket, badminton, squash, table tennis—he loved to play and always encouraged us to get involved. I played soccer and I enjoyed watching cricket, though I was never much of an athlete. I was a good swimmer, but team sports were not my specialty. My younger brother was the superstar of the family in that regard. I had learned to love sports as a fan. I liked the L.A. Lakers and avidly followed Pakistan's cricket team. Then, in 1996, I found my one true love: Manchester United.

I can't explain my unconditional allegiance to Manchester United; the intensity of my devotion grew to where no other sport mattered. A large part of it is the tradition, all the glorious history of the club. Part of it is its theatricality, the players, coaches, famous defections, classic matches, and moments of unexpected triumph.

Of the many deprivations I suffered in my first year of captivity, the absence of soccer in my life ranked pretty far down the list. When you spend your days praying to be allowed to take a shower or to be given an extra scrap of stale bread, interests such as soccer unsurprisingly find their place on a back burner.

Still, when Sohail said, "Brother, are you fond of sports?," I did a double take. Was this a trap of some sort? Was he planning to punish me for liking Manchester United, just another thing in this world that he considered *haram*?

It didn't matter because I couldn't possibly lie about my allegiance. "Yes. I'm a soccer fan."

Sohail looked me over and asked in a serious tone, "Who do you support?" You might have thought we were two scholars discussing the Holy Book. "Let me guess," he said. "Manchester City or Chelsea or Real Madrid."

Now I was worried. I couldn't lie about loving Manchester United, but the last thing I wanted was to find out that my guard, who literally held my life in his hands, was a Chelsea fan.

Then again, I always said I'm a Manchester United fan, do or die.

I took a deep breath. "If you love soccer, you can only love Manchester United."

Sohail narrowed his eyes at me. At first, I thought he was angry. But then I realized it was something else.

He didn't believe me.

Could it be, he seemed to be wondering, that he and this infidel supported the same soccer club?

"You're not a Manchester United fan," he said finally.

"Ask me anything!"

So, without hesitating, he asked a series of questions on the club's historical movement.

I answered accurately.

Sohail broke out in a childlike smile.

With that, our impromptu contest began, as we bantered back and forth like two crazed fans in the stands.

"Whose leg did Roy Keane break in Manchester City?" I asked.

"Håland," he answered without missing a beat.

We both broke into grins.

"Let me ask you this," I said. "Who scored the first-ever goal for Manchester United?"

At this, he threw up his hands and started to laugh. "You really *are* a soccer freak. Do you have any idea what's been happening in the last year and a half?"

"What do you think?" I looked around at my mud-walled room. "How could I possibly know?"

"Manchester City scored in the last minute and won the title last year."

I was horrified. Not Manchester City.

We commiserated in silence.

"Who won the Champions League?" I finally asked.

"Chelsea."

Another setback for my beloved Manchester United.

I realized I was having the most absurd conversation with the most absurd person in the most absurd place in the world.

We sat for a few more moments in silence. Then Sohail spoke those magical words:

"Wanna listen to a ManU match, mate?"

He brought in a small transistor radio. We sat side by side sharing one pair of earphones with the radio between us, tuned to the BBC broadcast of the game. I knew that, for Sohail, listening to the game was forbidden. If Muhammad Ali caught us, he would definitely beat me, but Sohail would also be in line for fifty lashes. This confirmed Sohail was nearly as die-hard a fan as I was.

Tears of joy ran down my cheeks listening to that first game on the radio. Those familiar sounds: the roar of the fans, the sounds of cheering, the crowd singing together, the names of all the players I adored. It was unbelievable. There I was, sitting in a mud room in the tribal territories, doing exactly what I might be doing if I were sitting at home in Lahore: enjoying a Manchester United game.

Of course, if I were home, I'd be watching on a big screen with all my friends gathered around, cheering, laughing, and enjoying ourselves. Instead, I was huddled up against my guard, listening on one earphone like this. I had never before in my life listened to a soccer match on the radio. It didn't matter. This was a taste of nostalgia. I knew that somewhere, miles away, my brother was likely watching the same game. Maybe he was thinking of me and feeling my absence. Perhaps he was even rooting by saying, "Win this one for Shabby!"

To top things off, Manchester United won the match.

**That moment felt like a visit from a dear old friend who** arrives unannounced. Someone who drops by without warning, and once you spend time with the person, only then do you realize how much you've missed the person as part of your life.

For me, that old friend was my old self. It was the person I'd left behind on a street in Lahore, the person whose name I had not heard since then. I was visited by Shabby T, the happy-go-lucky soccer fan, the carefree kid, the one with the ideal life that had all vanished in an instant.

When the game was over, Sohail put away the radio. This would now become our weekend ritual. Sohail would smuggle in the radio and we'd sit and listen together, stifling our cheers so as not to be found out.

For the rest of the week, it was business as usual.

The room. The chains. Soon enough, once I'd sufficiently healed from the drone strike, we were back to the torture as well.

# 23

In March of 2013, the torture resumed. I'd earned a few months of respite by virtue of nearly being killed in a drone attack and then contracting a near-fatal bout of malaria. It took months for me to get back to something resembling health. Once I was deemed fit by Muhammad Ali, he decided to start sending new videos to my family. This time he would up the ante.

Muhammad Ali's vacant life allowed him endless hours to contemplate his next horror movie where I was the victim and he was the ruthless tormentor.

One night he came into my room with a sinister expression and an evil grin. "Ahmed, tomorrow we will pull out your fingernails on your left hand."

I'm not sure what the rest of the people in the house thought of the screaming that came from my room. Their reaction wasn't foremost on my mind.

I understood enough about the objectives of their torture. The anticipation is often worse than the event. That is the real torture—imagining what is to come. That's why Muhammad Ali made a point of alerting me the night before. The difference now was that he wasn't trying to extract information from me or to break me. He aspired to be the Spielberg of horror films.

For Muhammad Ali's epic horror clips a numbing cocktail was injected into my fingertips as a painkiller. My uncontrollable, involuntary screams seemed to last forever, until I eventually passed out. I was brought back to consciousness by searing pain.

Back in Lahore my mother was in touch with the ISI. They put her in contact with a man who agreed at act as an intermediary.

Not long after, Muhammad Ali came to my room again

"Ahmed, tomorrow we will sew your mouth shut."

My day consisted of a strange mix. Unlike the endless desperation of 2012, when I'd spent most of my hours alone in a darkening spiral, the winter of 2013 was different. I'd been reintroduced to human comforts such as companionship, a kind word, a child's smile. I could even listen to Manchester United games! The radio reminded me of a world beyond my walls.

As Muhammad Ali's desperation grew, the torture became more aggressive and adventurous.

He lived up to his promise to sew my mouth shut.

Using a curved surgical needle, he crudely inserted six stitches, left in for three days, which meant no food or water for me. Besides the throbbing pain, this left me dehydrated, starved, and weak. Nearing the onset of winter, I was to experience the most brutal form of torture yet for Muhammad Ali's next video clip. Fearing the unknown, I was instructed to stand facing a wall with my shirt removed and my arms spread out over my head. This was the first of three assaults, which were deep cuts down my back with a shaving blade.

The first contact with the cold blade sent me into paralytic shock. I found it difficult to breathe.

Following the incisions, salt was rubbed on my wounds by Sohail.

After that torture, Abdul Aziz visited me in my room and brought balms to sooth my back. My days consisted of unthinkable atrocities, followed by gestures of kindness.

Amid Muhammad Ali's enthusiasm for his video productions, reckless decisions were taken. My mind would race with thoughts of gangrene and tetanus. In my horror I believed I would die of septicemia. The use of unsterilized blades, the crude pliers and knives, compounded by my squalid and unhygienic living conditions, were a perfect formula for an infection.

Next he had the guards dig a hole in the dirt floor that was deep enough for a man to stand in. I was lured into the hole, which was then filled with dirt up to my neck. Unable to move, I felt the dirt pressing against me as if it would crush my ribs. This torture was not about pain, but psychological torment. The effect is indescribable. This was the most excruciating torture yet. It's one thing to be subjected to pain, but pain can become familiar. Your body has defenses against pain. But to be immobilized, buried, unable to move or breathe. I thought I would go insane. When they finally dug me up, my skin was moist and wrinkled, hanging from the bone, as if I'd spent a year in a bath. I worried that it might fall off in great chunks right there.

The first time they did this to me, Muhammad Ali left me in the hole for an hour. The next time, for an afternoon. Then, for nearly a day.

When they dug me up the third time, it was as if they were unearthing a dead man. I felt as cold and lifeless as a corpse. I couldn't imagine what new effect Muhammad Ali thought these videos would have on my family. But reason had apparently long since stopped being any motivation for him.

Then, without warning, the torture stopped. It was all thanks to the intercession of a woman I'd only ever spoken to once, but whose mercy I will never, ever forget.

Aya Jaan was a strapping woman, six feet tall, with an imposing presence; a matriarch with an infectious laugh. She could be strict and harsh and then in a flash compassionate and affectionate. One thing was always clear: this was her house and she dictated the rules.

This was never more apparent to me than one day in the summer of 2013, when I was enduring a particularly horrific torture session.

Muhammad Ali had a harebrained scheme to videotape me after I was bitten by bees. He collected many bees in a jar from a fruit vendor's cart and brought them to my room.

The bees were dead for lack of oxygen in the jar.

He insisted on going ahead with his plan to film me. I sat crossed-legged in a pink hoodie on the cold floor in my drab, dank room. Sohail and a young fighter picked up the bees and started to poke me and sting me with then. Soon my face was swollen, as were my lips. I found it difficult to speak and was dragging a little; it had the desired visual effect, and I delivered a slurred message to my mother.

Suddenly all hell broke loose as a bee stung me in my scrotum. I nearly passed out with the pain. I was shivering and writhing around the room when Abdul Aziz ran in and brought me tweezers, and with my quivering hands I removed the stinger. The memory still makes me break out in a cold sweat.

For the next video, outside my room were Muhammad Ali, Sohail, Abdul Aziz, and a couple of bodyguards. With each video the intensity of torture had escalated. It seemed Muhammad Ali needed to amplify my pain to traumatize my mother. In this episode flesh was to be cut from my back and then fed to me. All caught on camera to horrify my family back in Lahore.

Abdul Aziz turned away from the sight of flesh, blood, and my desperate cries. He vomited uncontrollably.

To the other men, Abdul Aziz was weak. Not a freedom fighter as they believed they were. Horrified, Abdul Aziz, now measuring Muhammad Ali's deranged behavior and understanding he had crossed a line and was out of control, darted to Aya Jann.

Moments after, outside my room, I heard a sound I hadn't heard in years: the voice of an enraged woman giving everyone a piece of her mind.

Muhammad Ali rushed to calm her. I heard her authoritative voice in a rage as she gave him a dressing down. "You will not do this under my roof! This man is a guest in this house!"

Unbelievably, he complied.

This marked the end of the torture sequences. However events would unfold in the future, I would always be grateful to Aya Jaan for this act of mercy.

I will say one thing for my Uzbek captors. The men were cruel and savage, but they did listen when the matriarch laid down the law.

I constantly prayed that contact with my father-in-law would be severed, as after each of the few times he spoke to my captors, I got a sound thrashing. I was told this man knew nothing, he was not a stakeholder, and they didn't believe anything he said.

The persistent threatening calls to my mother along with the graphic videos were not delivering results, i.e., the release of twenty-eight terrorists and 4 billion rupees.

I was shocked to hear Muhammad Ali berating my father-in-law, calling him a nasty, egotistical, arrogant little man.

A bit rich, I felt, coming from Muhammad Ali, who displayed each of these characteristics and wore them proudly on his sleeve.

Once the torture ended, my healing began both mentally and physically.

The joy of Manchester United games saved my sanity. That single lifeline back to civilization kept me from going over the edge. As the seasons changed, I could glimpse the changes in the branches of the pomegranate tree as it came into bloom. I had the companionship of Abdul Aziz, who would fill in for Sohail as my guard. Abdul Aziz and I would sit and talk for hours in my room. A simple thing compared to the early days when I'd sit and talk endlessly to a spider. This was certainly an improvement. Abdul Aziz was the one person I'd met who might, I thought, have had a chance at a different life if he'd been born in different circumstances. It was only luck, I guess, that dictated that I'd been born to a prominent, successful family in Lahore, and he'd been born to a family of terrorists in Waziristan. He often asked me about my childhood and had me describe my various friends. I took great pains to communicate what each of them was like, as well as how much I loved and missed them.

One day, sitting in my room, he asked me, "If your friends met me, outside of this situation, do you think they would like me?"

I looked him over. I wanted to be honest. I owed him that, I felt. "Yes. I do. Especially if I told them how kind you've been to me."

This seemed to make him happy. He liked the notion that this different life, just beyond his grasp, might actually have a place for him.

The children's presence and energy were healing me. They would come several times a week for lessons in Urdu. Muhammad Ali instructed the guards to uncuff me whenever the children came in. I could walk freely around my room like a normal person. He even attempted to brighten up my room, albeit for the children's sake. It's common in that area of Pakistan for people to hang large paper coverings over their mud walls to limit the dust and enliven the room. Muhammad Ali, for example, had a huge paper covering in his own room that featured, of all things, row after row of bright green bottles of Gatorade. I knew this because I had repeatedly been tortured in this room. As the nails on my left hand were pulled out, I was staring at Gatorade bottles. How's that for product placement?

The paper Muhammad Ali brought into my room to cover the walls featured a different image. I didn't get to choose, of course, and nobody consulted me. I was just happy for any change of scenery. Two guards nailed up the covering: a large, blown-up photo from a Windows screen saver. It even said COPYRIGHT WINDOWS at the bottom and described what the photo was:

A landscape shot of Montalcino, Italy.

That's the medieval town where I'd spent my summers with my father as a boy.

After the guards left, I stood and stared at my paper Montalcino. It seemed impossible. They could have hung literally anything here. They could have hung pictures of Gatorade. They had no idea that I had any connection to Tuscany. Yet now I could look every day at the place where I'd spent all those treasured summers with my father. The place where he'd educated me and introduced me to museums. Where he'd lectured me on art and history. Where we'd laughed as he lounged by the swimming pool, his favorite place on earth.

This wasn't a ticket home. But it definitely felt like an escape.

This time, no wall had fallen on me and I hadn't survived another air strike. But once again, as I looked over this unlikely Italian vista from a room in a remote village in Pakistan, I had the feeling that I'd been the beneficiary of the unlikeliest of small miracles.

# 24

As spring approached, the torture stopped, allowing my body to heal. The children were with me a lot of the time. I watched as the top of the pomegranate tree bloomed. This, coupled with the company of the children, made it a relatively happy period.

I had fallen so far into darkness that even a sliver of light seemed like daybreak to me.

I missed my family and friends desperately. I missed my former existence in Lahore, which had now become a blurred haze of what seemed a distant past.

However, at times complete hopelessness eclipsed sanity. It was then that I would find my father's reassuring hand on my shoulder, lifting my demoralized and broken spirit and guiding me with his accumulated wisdom. On many occasions this kept me going. I was fed up, angry, rude, and highly provocative. I refused to be submissive, taunting my captors to do their worst. Living or dying meant nothing to me. In response, their knee-jerk reaction was to abuse, kick, and beat me further. Abba guided me to stop being obstinate and to concentrate on how to get out of this situation alive. If I stubbornly provoked my kidnappers, the odds of success would be against me. Abba reminded me to keep my wits about me and not sink to the level of these barbarians. This sound advice served me well.

I had been gone for almost two years. Sometimes when I lay awake at night in Mir Ali and tried to remember the voice of my wife, calling my name, calling me back to bed on that fateful morning before I was kidnapped, I found that I could not remember it. I tried to recall her face. It had been so long since I'd seen her. Each time I struggled to reconstruct her in my mind, I realized that, while I remained devoted, I had begun to let the memory of her go. What I wanted most for her was happiness, and if that happiness meant she would move on from me, perhaps it was for the best.

During my days, I settled into the routine of the household. The Urdu lessons continued. I read my Quran and said my prayers. My father came to me in my dreams at night, and even during the day we had meaningful conversations. I felt his presence. He told me to stay brave. He was my constant source of fortitude. Strange as it sounds, he was there. I felt him with me all the time, unwavering till the end. He made sure I was not alone in my darkest moments. I know that he gave his life for something big, but I also believe he died to save me.

About eight hundred days into my kidnapping I marked a change in my living conditions: I had the company of Sohail, with whom I had developed an equation of sorts. We were not friends; he was still the same person who'd held my hands down while my nails were ripped out, who had literally rubbed salt in my wounds. Regardless, we became companions, sharing a common interest in soccer and a love for ManUnited, reminiscing about classic games and favorite players.

He slowly opened up to me about himself. He told me that, growing up in rural Uzbekistan, he had never had a female friend. His culture forbade it. Naturally, he was bewildered by the idea of women. He was married yet shared little or no emotional intimacy with his wife. He was unable to process that I'd attended a coeducational school, that my sister was a strong and courageous public figure and my mother a strong and formidable woman. Some of the longest-lasting friendships I had were with women, with whom I spoke as freely as I did with any male friends. To Sohail, such a relationship was not just impossible to conduct, it was unthinkable. I realized this was just another way in which a myopic view of the world had punished him, leaving him a poorer person.

I also discovered that, even though Sohail's childhood had been vastly different from mine, he'd been just as entranced by Western culture. I tried to imagine young Sohail, sitting cross-legged in his mud house in Uzbekistan, watching the antics of American sitcoms on some archaic television set. This fascination with Western culture had even lingered into his adulthood, so from time to time he'd bring in a pirated American movie for us to watch together. In Mir Ali, which is administered by the Taliban, watching movies was considered okay, and pirated DVDs were readily available in the local market. The only people forbidden from watching movies were the joyless Uzbeks. But Sohail couldn't resist. He'd smuggle in a DVD and stick it into an old laptop, and we'd sit together, side by side, sharing a pair of earphones, watching the screen. It was our own little secret drive-in theater, with an enthusiastic audience of two.

One night he brought in *The Wolverine*, which we both enjoyed. Looking back, I laugh and think that Sohail and I were a bizarre version of Siskel and Ebert, watching these movies on our little laptop in a mud hut, then giving them a thumbs-up or thumbs-down. Usually we agreed, unless there was anything suggestive about the movie. In that case, Sohail could not deal with it. We watched the *Fast and Furious* movie that was filmed in Brazil, and each time a scantily clad woman came into view, Sohail would get flustered and lunge forward to cover the screen with his hands. I found it hilarious. This was the first time I'd seen anything even vaguely risqué in over two years, other than the woman on the box of soap that Abdul Aziz had brought me and then torn up in my face.

On another night, Sohail told me he'd acquired a copy of a recent award-winning American movie. It was *Zero Dark Thirty*, about the American mission to kill Osama bin Laden in Pakistan. I was surprised Sohail would want to watch this movie, given it's all about the killing of one of his great heroes by his sworn enemy the Americans. But Sohail was interested in the film and wanted to know the story. Once it ended, he was agitated. He insisted, "It's all bullshit. It's all fabricated Western propaganda!," which is what he also believed about 9/11. He and his fellow mujahideen always claimed 9/11 was a lie, an American hoax, engineered as justification for attacking Afghanistan and the rising Islamic caliphate. The Uzbeks had a negative bias against Arabs and refused to admit that a crew of mostly Saudi Arabians could have pulled off such an attack.

"This is a lie!" Sohail said about *Zero Dark Thirty*, speaking quietly so that no one else in the house would hear.

"It's not," I said. "It's a true story!"

Adamant, Sohail insisted this was nothing but blasphemy. Nevertheless, we watched it all the way to the end.

After Aya Jaan forbade any further torture, Abdul Aziz felt empowered and instructed Sohail to uncuff me. In an authoritative manner Abdul Aziz took control over the quality of my conditions. At night I remained chained to the floor; during the day I could walk freely around my room, which felt liberating after being contained like an animal. The children often came to play in my room. The break in monotony of both the children and my routine was welcome. It reenergized me, constantly reminding me of my family at home.

Sometimes Sohail would leave his radio, allowing me to listen to news of the outside world, on the condition I did so with earphones. I remember one day in the spring of 2013, listening to the BBC world report, hoping to hear soccer scores, when a particular news story struck me. The BBC announcer told an unbelievable tale, about three young women in Cleveland, in the United States. A neighbor had heard one of them screaming for help from behind a locked door. When he kicked the door down, the woman escaped and called the police. The police arrived and found two other women detained in the house. All three had been held captive in that house for ten years. Reporters were calling the story incredible, unbelievable. The rescue of Amanda Berry, Gina DeJesus, and Michelle Knight was heralded as a miracle. To me, it sounded relatable. Listening to the story on the radio, I started to weep.

I wasn't weeping for my own captivity, or because they'd escaped and I was still a hostage. These were tears of joy, celebrating the women's escape. God had certainly heard their prayers. I didn't know them, but felt happy for their freedom as if they'd been my own sisters.

**For me, life continued in Mir Ali. I was like a forgotten man.** Not only by my family, I had begun to imagine, but also forgotten as an unusual presence in the household. I'd been absorbed into the simple rhythm of this home. You might think I dreamed of freedom daily or plotted my escape, drawing plans in the dirt like a prisoner in a movie, but in reality, in North Waziristan, I had no place to escape to. Freedom was a via a dusty path still hundreds of miles away; decamping in the dead of the night was not an option as I had no clue as to where I was. Muhammad Ali allowed me more access around the compound as I knew all too well that I was safer under his watch than in the bazaar. Escaping would mean one of three things. Were I to plead my case to the locals, they would either kill me or hand me over to Muhammad Ali for a ransom or, worst of all, take me hostage and start the entire process all over again.

With the easing of restrictions, my mental and physical health improved.

I was better off waiting and clinging to the unlikely hope that my family would make a breakthrough in the negotiations. But I often wondered how a settlement would come about given the outrageous demands.

When I returned to Lahore in March 2016, my dear and fiercely loyal childhood friend Rafael Rasheed asked me seriously if I had gone "homeland" on life. Puzzled, I asked what was "homeland." He was referring to the protagonist in the television series, *Homeland*, who suffered from the famous

Stockholm syndrome during his captivity, brainwashed into siding with his enemy. Assuring Rafael there was no chance of that, I told him to wait for my page-turning book.

My animated conversations with Muhammad Ali over religion had become more fierce, more volatile. My restored confidence as well as my shred of self-respect meant I was no longer scared of verbally sparring with him. He had already stripped me of everything. He had done his worst.

In fact, I had begun to witness chinks in Muhammad Ali's armor.

As I studied my Quran, I became more confident in my understanding of it. Quick to challenge his twisted interpretations, I could quote chapter and verse back to him just as quickly as he'd quote them to me. We argued often over disputed passages, with him always taking the side that the Quran advocates all manner of violence, while in my reading it preaches tolerance and peace. He loved to hold court and spout opinions; he was used to being surrounded by nodding acolytes. I was no yes-man. Looking back, I believe the secret reason he returned time after time to our conversations was because he wasn't used to having someone challenge his warped views.

**Among the most bewildering visits from Muhammad Ali** were the ones in which he discussed his future plans. He would spend hours explaining to me the complicated politics of the local extremist organizations, with their infighting, jostling for power, and complicated internal politics. I'd never paid much attention to the details of that sort of thing when I lived in Lahore, the hows and whys of who was killing whom out in the wilderness. I was too busy working and planning my future. Now I'd become a homeschooled expert in the intricacies of terror organizations. I knew who was allied with whom, who hated whom, and why. Muhammad Ali was a rising star in the IMU hierarchy and clearly had his eye on a leadership role, which was currently held by Usman Ghazi. To that end, Muhammad Ali had cooked up various terror schemes, some of which were already in motion. Those were insane enough, but the real treat was when he'd come to tell me about his delusional plans for the days when the new Islamic caliphate had defeated Western civilization and conquered the world.

One day, he charged into my room in one of his more exuberant moods, ready to spar. "You've traveled. Tell me, where are the most beautiful women in the world?"

Muhammad Ali's exposure to the world was limited to Pakistan and Afghanistan. He knew that I had traveled all over Europe and America. He wanted to make a point, clearly, but first he wanted my honest opinion.

The question was laughable, without a sensible answer. "I don't know. Brazil? It's famous for beautiful women."

"Too far away," he said, as if we were planning a road trip.

I thought of Italy and the many summers I spent there. "Rome?"

"Yes. Rome is the way." He started babbling a ridiculous tale of how, when the great Islamic caliphate was established and Europe had fallen, he'd make his new home in Rome. He'd subjugate and rape all the women he met. "I'll make the pope's residence the place for my whores."

The Vatican, a jewel of modern civilization, was to be reduced to a madman's palace.

I stared at him in disbelief, having visited the Vatican with my parents and understanding the security and protocol afforded to the pope. Muhammad Ali's plan would sound preposterous to any sane person. As his rambling continued, I put my guard up, controlling any urge to respond, fearing his displeasure, which could lead to new forms of physical violence.

The stench of his verbal diarrhea filled my mind with anger:

*Do you understand that I've actually* been *to Rome? What do you think they'd say if you and your so-called warriors showed up in your dirty clothes and your ridiculous beards? They would laugh at you! You think you're going to live in the Vatican one day? Are you serious? You're delusional, man.*

I realized to a man such as Muhammad Ali, the Rome he was describing may as well have been the Land of Oz. He had never seen it and never would. It reminded me of a short story I'd read, "The Secret Life of Walter Mitty." Muhammad Ali had told himself grandiose tales of conquest, indulged in absurd fantasies, whereas in reality the gulf between a lunatic such as him and actual civilization was unbridgeable. He was nothing but a lone madman, ranting in a mud hut. No doubt he had the power to hurt people and ruin lives. Mine, for starters, in part by forcing me to be his captive audience.

I might have to listen, but that didn't mean I had to agree. What more could he do? He'd taken strips of flesh out of my back! I'd survived.

He could take away my privileges. I'd eaten little else but goat fat for an entire year. I'd endured it. I'd survived.

Kill me.

At that point I would have said, "Go ahead. Do it. What life will I be missing? Sitting here and listening to your idiocy? I'd rather sit at my father's side in the afterlife. I'll go to him. So, kill me and set me free."

Muhammad Ali had already taken everything from me that was true. But in doing so, he'd given me one thing back. He'd given me the freedom to tell him what a fool he was.

Among the insufferable periods with Muhammad Ali, particularly unpalatable were those when he berated the women in my family. My mother, my sister Shehrbano, were constantly being accused of an immoral Western lifestyle. His most frequent target was Maheen, and he insisted that her outward appearance masked the evil that lay underneath.

**As 2013 came to a close, Muhammad Ali became involved** in other endeavors. He'd orchestrated three more kidnappings since my own that had netted him three hundred thousand dollars in ransom. Not a fortune, and not anywhere close to what he stubbornly believed he could extract from my family, but enough to bankroll his continuing ambitions. I never met or saw his other victims. They were held at different safe houses. I would hear about them from Muhammad Ali, who loved to boast to me about his exploits.

He'd also organized several attacks on army soldiers stationed in or around Mir Ali. This was the life of an extremist: plot an attack, feel momentary triumph, and endure the repercussions. Our lives in Mir Ali were marked by constant skirmishes between members of the IMU and soldiers in the Pakistani army. Militia fighters would attack an army truck or blow up a check post, and the army would retaliate by shelling a village or sending helicopters in to launch rocket strikes. This was commonplace, the stuff of everyday life, and eventually I, just like the men and women and even the little children around me, learned to live as though hearing the sounds of rockets and gunfire was as natural as hearing birdsong in the trees. The fighting outside rarely affected life in the house I was being held in. If anything, the strangest thing for me was watching the children, such as little Fatimah, who could play unfazed by the distant sounds of mortar fire or missile strikes. To the children, this was just the soundtrack to their world.

In November 2013, this landscape changed. The constant conflict that characterized our lives escalated to actual war. As with any war, there would be casualties, and consequences none of us could foresee.

# 25

On November 1, 2013, one of the Taliban's most valuable assets was killed in a targeted drone strike. Hakimullah Mehsud, a wanted terrorist in Pakistan, carried a large bounty and an additional $5 million reward for accurate information leading to his capture. He had been living under the radar, lying low, undetected in the village of Miranshah, a few miles from Mir Ali.

In an earlier drone strike on May 29, 2013, Wali-ur-Rehman, the second-in-command to the TTP (Tehreek-e-Taliban) leader Hakimullah Mehsud, was killed in North Waziristan.

The ISI had facilitated a negotiation between my mother and Wali-ur-Rehman to secure my release. Serious progress had been made, with, for the first time, concrete discussions with an achievable target. Sadly his death put an end to my negotiations.

No one was mourning Wali-ur-Rehman, only the loss of an opportunity.

The systematic elimination of their top leadership infuriated the TTP, prompting a series of deadly attacks targeting different cities of Pakistan.

Muhammad Ali considered himself a big deal, though I knew he wasn't an important enough threat that his house would merit a targeted attack. Whether the Pakistani government would think twice before shelling a house that they knew I was in, I was not sure. It was made clear to me that the government had long since given up on finding a way to secure my release. Everything I heard from my family about the lack of support from the government confirmed my suspicions. Only later did I find out that my mother had had to distance herself from the government to lower the Uzbeks' level of expectation.

The fatal drone strikes that killed Hakimullah Mehsud and Wali-ur-Rehman had a direct impact on the negotiations about me. For one, the fighting in and around Mir Ali would intensify as the Pakistani Taliban retaliated. The group put into place plans for an ambitious and deadly attack that would make worldwide headlines and set off a series of events that would upend my world.

The other significant development was Muhammad Ali, my captor, was to get a promotion.

My mother, now desperate to establish a channel of communication with Muhammad Ali, was advised by Maheen's uncle, a resident of and practicing physician in Khyber Pakhtunkhwa, to approach Maulana Sami ul-Haq, in Akora Khattak. He was the head of one of the largest madrassas in Pakistan. The infamous Maulana put my father-in-law and my mother in touch with a leader of the Haqqani network, Haji Khalil-ur-Rehman Haqqani. He helped to reengage my family with the Uzbeks.

My mother had been cautioned by the ISI, noting this

man's lack of credibility, insisting the Haqqani network had shifted loyalties and were now considered marked men.

In December 2013, Usman Majid, one of the men involved in my kidnapping, returned to Mir Ali after a long hiatus and was reunited with Muhammad Ali. Usman Majid fled Pakistan after my abduction and traveled to Norway, where he took refuge in a migrant camp. He was subsequently identified, deported, and found his way back to Waziristan. He arrived with news of the outside world: the war between the various extremists in North Waziristan and the Pakistani army was about to intensify. Mir Ali would no longer be safe for Muhammad Ali's family, or for me, though I was certainly the last of Muhammad Ali's or anyone else's concerns.

Usman Majid was accorded a hero's welcome; he held court in the compound, enthralling the simpletons with embellished stories of his conquests. The nauseating tales continued for three days.

Just after daybreak on December 18, 2013, as Sohail arrived with a cup of tea, a deafening explosion occurred, one louder and more powerful than anything we had heard or felt before. The blast caused the great warrior Usman Majid to urinate in his *shalwar*. I glanced at Sohail, who looked back with a smirk, as Usman Majid was exposed as the pathetic coward he actually was.

The TTP and al-Qaeda had planned a suicide attack on the army camp in Mir Ali. The objective was to cause maximum devastation. Packed with high-powered explosives, a truck posing as an army vehicle, driven by suicide bombers, was detonated inside the camp, leaving behind carnage.

In retaliation for this incident Mir Ali was now blitzed by the army, exposing its inhabitants to days of shock waves, further revealing Usman Majid's true nature.

By a process of elimination Muhammad Ali had been promoted as the IMU's new head of intelligence, effectively making him the second-in-command. He had control over all tactical operations and was part of an ambitious plan on the horizon. Now the TTP planned a joint operation with the IMU, using voluntary recruits. Training for this operation was conducted at Muhammad Ali's command. With Quranic verses he brainwashed them to support their ultimate sacrifice.

Muhammad Ali embraced his new role within the IMU and became a powerful mufti for the group. He was revered for his extensive (if warped) knowledge of Islamic scripture. I'd often hear him in an adjoining room, expounding endlessly to his recruits as he prepared to send them off to certain death. His interpretation of the scripture was perverse, but I had to admit he had an incredible, almost impressive, ability to indoctrinate their innocent minds with his zealotry. I could understand why these impressionable recruits were falling under his spell. He'd come from a similar background as many of these young men and had traveled the same road as them. He'd been desperately poor as a child and raised to be full of malevolence, so he knew how to stoke hatred in their hearts. He took advantage of their weakness and preyed on their minds, persuading them to become suicide bombers. As I heard him talk, he reminded me of a cult leader—charismatic, fearsome, and beguiling to the weak-minded and the desperate.

After receiving news of the coming offensive, Muhammad Ali moved up his plans to have the women and children of his household transported out of Mir Ali. They would undertake the grueling but necessary journey to the Shawal Valley, about sixty miles southwest of Mir Ali.

As the women and children packed up, Aya Jaan pulled me aside. This was the first time we ever spoke; the first time we made eye contact. She wore a veil but her eyes were visible to me. I could see she was crying.

Abdul Aziz translated the conversation. She emotionally said she was sorry I'd been tortured and mistreated. Had it been up to her, my treatment would have been different. She said that during my stay at her home, she'd considered me a son. She'd done all she could to protect me, but now she had to focus on saving her own children. As her eyes welled up, she said her heart was heavy at the prospect of leaving me at the mercy of Muhammad Ali. "You are brave," she said, with Abdul Aziz translating her words carefully. "And you are alive for a reason."

I respectfully thanked her, with Abdul Aziz now translating my words. I said how grateful I was that she'd interceded on my behalf, and how, in her kindness, she'd helped me rediscover my humanity. I told her I would never forget her compassion and all that she had done for me.

As we stood up to say farewell, our one and only conversation completed, both of us were in tears.

By early 2014, the women and children had been relocated to Shawal, leaving only the men behind. The night sky was lit up by jets unleashing their fury, and the sounds of their bombs were deafening. I'd lie awake and wonder if the next bombing run would find us. A sense of complete powerlessness comes with lying in the dark waiting for death to come from above. For years, I'd been at the mercy of men who held my life in their hands. Now, it felt as if we were all at the mercy of the wrath of an irate God who thundered over mercilessly annihilating everything in his path.

During the day Muhammad Ali's young army spent their

waking hours training with Kalashnikovs, firing rockets, and making propaganda videos. They prepared for an attack perfectly aware that active duty was a call away. Readying themselves to wage their jihad in Mir Ali if required. I knew all about their plans through Muhammad Ali. Often his plans never came to fruition and his grand schemes were forgotten or replaced with new ambitious ideas to brag about.

One day, fed up with his boasting, I said, "Look at you. You are only here because of me. I'm your biggest accomplishment."

When I said this, he didn't get angry or enraged. He actually smiled. I think he liked it when I stood up to him. Possibly because he knew that, no matter what I did, I was still at his mercy.

**In May 2014, the TTP kidnapped a Chinese cyclist on a solo** journey through Pakistan from Lahore to Tibet. The abduction prompted global headlines, pressuring the Chinese government to secure his immediate release. This happened hundreds of kilometers away from us, but it spurred a renewed offensive by the army, which meant our tenuous situation got even worse. More jets. More bombs. More air strikes.

I realized that we were now in the midst of a full-scale war. Everything prior to this had simply been a skirmish. Jets had never before been involved. Muhammad Ali's recruits had been moved out to Quetta, in Balochistan, closer to Karachi, a sleeper cell waiting to be activated. Sohail, Muhammad Ali, and I worked tirelessly to turn my cell into a pit. We dug out the floor to a depth deep enough for us to take shelter. The house was now largely empty. At the sound of an approaching jet, we'd rush for cover, huddling securely in the makeshift bomb shelter, waiting for danger to pass. I often wondered how my life had brought me here. Hiding with my captors, fearing the bombs of my own government, in a town that had been evacuated of all but the craziest and most dangerous of men. Lahore seemed far away, and my old life more like a faded memory.

In the aftermath of the Mir Ali bombing, the TTP and the IMU put into motion their plan. On June 8, 2014, they attacked the Jinnah International Airport in Karachi. Ten militants, armed with automatic rifles and suicide vests, disguised as airport security guards, stormed the airport just before midnight and murdered twenty-six people.

On the night of the attack, Muhammad Ali was ecstatic. I'd never seen him so elated. He brought each of us mobile phones so we could watch the breaking news reports live. "We brought them to their knees!" he kept saying, as though this was the culmination of all his wildest dreams. His family was on the run, his hometown was in ruins, his house had been turned into a wartime bunker, he'd sent ten people to their deaths and caused the deaths of dozens more, yet he felt that he had won a great victory.

In a way, he had. The attack made international headlines. It was his life's greatest accomplishment.

The Karachi airport attack set in motion events that would mark a terrifying new stage of my captivity and ultimately lead me to a most improbable endgame.

First, we'd have to evacuate Mir Ali. If Muhammad Ali thought that Mir Ali had felt the wrath of the Pakistan army before the airport attack, it was nothing compared to what was yet to come. If the mujahideen killed a soldier, the army would slaughter their families. If they killed dozens of innocent people in a bombing, the armed forces would carpet-bomb their whole village out of existence. This made no sense to me and only reaffirmed what I already understood. Muhammad Ali was a lunatic who didn't fear violence, he lived for it. I knew he'd been digging his own grave from the first day we met. The trouble was, in his digging that grave, I believed, I was helplessly handcuffed to his fate.

The airport attackers were identified as Uzbeks, the men trained by Muhammad Ali in Mir Ali. By undertaking this mission their lives had been wasted and death was their only legacy.

Pakistan has suffered a spate of terrorist activity since 9/11. The government's decision to aid the U.S. forces in its fight in Afghanistan had angered Taliban fractions, who had mercilessly punished their fellow Pakistanis in senseless retaliation. This had become the brutal reality of life in Pakistan, a country now plagued with terrorism. But the Karachi airport attack spurred a national call for a counteroffensive. Within days of the attack, army jets were flying over Miran Shah, unleashing wave after wave of bombings. The army targeted IMU hideouts in a thirty-five-mile span from Mir Ali to Datta Khel. This was the official start of a military operation in North Waziristan dubbed Zarb-e-Azb, "a sharp and cutting strike," which officially commenced on June 15, 2014. The objective was to flatten the whole place. It severely dismembered several extremist organizations, including the IMU, who took refuge in Afghanistan with me in tow. The operation displaced hundreds of thousands of people from North Waziristan, a desperately poor area whose tribal people had long been caught between the extremists exploiting the lawlessness of this region and the government forces unable to root the extremists out.

In the wake of the Karachi airport attack, the army settled

on a new tactic to scorch the earth. Flatten the villages, bomb the mountains, and worry about sorting through the corpses later.

There was no safe place for the Uzbeks to hide; the army was now determined to eliminate every last one of them.

**This was the start of the final phase of my captivity.** I didn't know it then, but our frantic retreat from Mir Ali now tied my fortunes inextricably to that of my pursued captor, which would lead us out of Pakistan and into Afghanistan. It would ultimately lead me toward freedom.

But first, the Shawal Valley.

Sohail, Usman Majid, a scraggly group of IMU fighters, and I made our way to the valley, while Muhammad Ali stayed behind to regroup. He entrusted Sohail with my custody, and we set off on a hundred-mile journey from Mir Ali to Shawal.

Before we left, Muhammad Ali took me aside. "I won't have to kill you now, Ahmed. Look around. The elements will bring about your death."

I wasn't sure if he meant this as a promise, a warning, or a threat.

# 26

The journey over the Miran Shah road from Mir Ali to Shawal stretches over sixty miles, and it took us nearly four hours to arrive. As we drove, I thought that under different circumstances this would have been an exciting excursion to one of the most remote and beautiful places in Pakistan. The scenery was green and deceptively peaceful, though the road was unpaved. The terrain is inhospitable for troops to move and operate in, with thickly forested and foliaged valleys, blanketed in snow for most of the year. Especially in winter, the valley is sparsely populated by Wazir tribes, and up until 2004 it was completely out of the administrative control of the Pakistani government.

There's not much in the way of commercial development, and nothing resembling a town. We passed maybe two or three small truck stops for long-haul cargo carriers and scattered stores for provisions. Compared to Shawal, Mir Ali had been a buzzing metropolis.

We had been issued clear instructions to hide out and wait for Muhammad Ali. We had no place to stay and no idea of his schedule.

We did, however, have a tent.

Sohail and I made camp halfway up a mountain on rocky, uneven terrain. The objective was to conceal ourselves not just from military raids but from curious locals. We did our best to stay out of sight and not attract attention. Being in a tent on a mountainside meant we could maintain a low profile and be mobile enough to relocate if necessary. But living in a tent on a mountainside also had its drawbacks. On the first night, it was impossible to get any sleep at all because of the sharp rocks, so I lay in the cold night air and mulled over my options. There were none.

Once daybreak came, Sohail and I excavated several layers of hard rock, then resettled our tent and our basic bedding on softer earth.

The direct sun was harsh yet cool. The military offensive that we'd traveled to escape didn't seem far away at all. As we dug, we would occasionally hear bombs being dropped on the mountains all around us and the earth below us shook.

We explored our surroundings to get a better understanding of the area. A trail passed our campsite and led to the top of the mountain, to a school. The modest building was full of life. To pass time Sohail and I would sit close to its periphery.

A week later while Sohail and I were enjoying the warm sun close to our camp, we heard the roar of passing jets. I dreaded the sound and had learned to fear it in my bones. I knew instinctively to run for cover. Before we heard any explosion, before we could even move, we were both violently flung through the air in a shower of rubble. The force of the explosion preceded even the noise. Your world collapses long before you hear the sound.

The jet strikes we'd been running from had found us.

Catapulted forward, Sohail and I tumbled down the side of the mountain, with debris raining down on us. The jet roar subsided. Shell-shocked and deafened, we rose to our feet, checking for injuries. We scrambled back to the top of the mountain to ascertain the damage.

Where the school had been was now death and destruction. The building was gone, with only a deep crater in its place. The surrounding terrain was littered with the remains of women's and children's bodies, seared bits and bloodied chunks scattered across the grass. I had never before seen the likes of this stomach-churning sight. I felt sick. By this time I had seen gruesome injuries and plenty of blood, some of it my own. For the first time I understood what the words *collateral damage* really meant. Of everything I saw during my captivity, this image may be the one that still haunts me the most.

**This was not to be the last of the air strikes. They esca-**lated. Jets roared and streaked across the sky several times a day in Shawal, the pounding of bombs shaking the earth. Having survived a drone strike, I am often asked how I feel about using drones as a method of war. I don't condone them, yet I've seen the alternative, which is indiscriminate carpet-bombing, which shakes you to your core.

At night, as we tried to sleep, I was haunted by the noise of jet engines. The jets didn't fly at night, but the thunderous sound of them tearing through the sky was the soundtrack to my nightmares. One day as I was sitting outside my tent, I looked up to see four veiled women coming up the trail toward our camp. I was alarmed. Who could be coming to find us? What had we done to attract their attention?

Terrified, I leaped to my feet, realizing I'd been spotted. Among them was a statuesque woman gesturing.

As I turned my back to the women and prepared to escape, I heard the sound of two children. I knew that laughter. I couldn't believe it. I turned to look back at the approaching party and nearly cried when I did. It was Muhammad Tahir and Fatimah, running to greet me. They scurried up and wrapped their little arms around my legs. The tall and heavy woman in the hajib who labored behind them was Aya Jaan, accompanied, I saw now, by Abdul Aziz and three other women. It felt like a family reunion.

The rest of the little children followed behind, and soon they'd all caught up with Sohail and me. They had come in search of us after hearing of our arrival in the valley, to graciously invite us into their humble abode. After several weeks of sleeping on the mountain, I was ready to return to a home, albeit one with mud walls.

Sohail and I settled into our new home. The modest building had walls and a roof, both improvements on our mountainside tent. We no longer had to sleep on rocky ground. The air strikes were increasing in frequency and intensity. Every time we heard the roar of jets, we huddled together with the children to take cover. As these strikes became more routine, we agreed on safe zones away from the house where we would run to. As a bomb fell nearby, the entire house creaked. I could see the mud walls straining to stay up under the relentless attacks.

As the household lay asleep in the dead of one night, I felt myself thrown from my bed.

Once more, the impact came before the sound.

The bomb had struck nearby. I knew more bombs would fall and likely bring down the house around us.

I did not think that this was my chance to run for freedom. I did not think how strange it was that after all my time in captivity, over three years now, my fate was so inextricably entangled with the family of the man who'd kidnapped me.

I didn't think of escape.

I thought of saving the lives of those innocent children.

A mixture of fear and adrenaline made me frantic. Every instinct told me to run from the house as fast as I could so I had one thought: *Run.* Then another thought: *Everyone in this house who doesn't exit will die.*

I found myself sprinting even before my feet hit the ground. I hurriedly ran out toward the designated safe zone in the bushes, where the women were already hiding. Even at a time such as this, I dared not look at them as they were still adjusting their clothes and veils. The bombs fell closer and closer. In this chaos and commotion I realized some children had been left behind. Abdul Aziz rushed toward me with an infant in each arm, his face white with panic. In all the confusion, Fatimah and Muhammad Tahir were still in the house.

Abdul Aziz turned to me with terror in his eyes, ready to plead with me to retrieve the two before the house was hit. I was already charging back toward them. I'd never done anything so counterintuitive in all my life. Completely abandoning self-preservation, I never gave my safety a second thought. It was all instinct. I could not leave those kids behind to perish.

As I struggled over the rough ground, my body was flung to the ground with each new impact. I scrabbled back to my feet and made my way into the house. I found Muhammad

Tahir right away, sitting stunned and wide-eyed on the bed in his room like a deer caught in headlights. I searched frantically for Fatimah, then found her too, paralyzed with fear under her bed. There was no time for explanations or directions. No time even to calm their fears. I just picked up Tahir in my left arm and Fatima in my right and ran as fast as I could. With bombs and shells exploding behind us, I carried them both back to the refuge of the huddled group. We sat there together, relatively safe in our retreat zone in the trees, as the bombs pounded what was left of the village and our mud house, which finally crumpled in clouds of dirt and debris.

**The next day was spent clearing an area on the side of the** mountain that would be home to our tents. Despite it being a makeshift arrangement I was grateful we had all survived and was happy to be reunited and together with the children.

Though Aya Jaan and Abdul Aziz were both part of the organization that had kidnapped me, from their little acts of kindness to me I'd developed a fondness for them. Several times they thanked me for rescuing the children.

In the weeks following the destruction of the mud hut, Muhammad Ali arrived with the last of the IMU fighters. He appeared forlorn and deflated after what he considered to be the greatest triumph of his life, the Karachi airport attack; he along with his family were now once again on the run.

When Muhammad Ali arrived, his family rushed to greet him. They couldn't wait to tell him about the night of the air strikes and how close we'd all been to death. Abdul Aziz explained with generous praise how I had rushed back into the house to save Muhammad Ali's children. He was neither grateful nor touched. To the contrary, he angrily dismissed my actions, then sneered deadpan, "He only did it to win your favor and save his own neck."

One night, as we sat outside our tents, Muhammad Ali began talking about his enemies, how these infidels had driven us into the mountains.

After weeks of dodging air strikes, sleeping on rocks, and watching his kids cower in fear at every bomb blast, I snapped, "The tragedy of all this is that you rant against your unknown enemies and blame them for all your misfortune, but the atrocities against your women and children are a direct result of your actions. They are bombed because of you. The army attacks because of you. You sent your fighters to the Karachi airport. You kill women and children."

"We must kill the women and children. It's very important. That way we strike them at their core."

"You're delusional!" I yelled, exasperated. "It says in the Quran you never fight a woman or a child!"

I sensed his rage. He tried to speak but I cut him off. "Every word spoken that goes against the Quran is null and void! Even you know that. Yet all your words are against the Quran."

He stood up, speechless, and resorted to the only tactic he still had. He kicked me. Then he left me to lie in the dirt.

Writhing in pain, I lay there and understood that for Muhammad Ali this was as close to an admission of failure as he would ever come.

**I didn't know it then, but Shawal Valley was considered** the final objective of the army's Operation Zarb-e-Azb. Because the valley is so treacherous, its slopes so inaccessible and its rocky terrain so inhospitable to advancing troops, Shawal was considered by the Pakistani army to be the toughest territory to be "cleansed." They weren't wrong; Muhammad Ali had sent us here to remain under the radar for a reason. With winter approaching and the nights growing colder and the air raids getting more unpredictable and more destructive, it became clear to us that even Shawal was too unsafe. Muhammad Ali arbitrarily decided we would relocate across the mountains to Afghanistan.

The plan was to send off an advance party of women and children, followed by the rest of us. This meant the family and I would once began be separated, but in my heart I was certain we would meet again. If I'd learned anything about Aya Jaan and her brood, it's that they were survivors.

My heart, however, was heavy for a different reason. I felt deep in my bones that if we left Pakistan, I might never return. It was as if I were saying a final goodbye to everything: my home, my life, my family. I had no hope that my family could track me down in Afghanistan or broker a deal. For the first time, bereft of hope, I gave up the notion that I would ever return to my home in Lahore. This was my life now. It was beyond my control.

# 27

In the mid-1980s my father added a swimming pool to our home. It became the center of our activity. There, along with swimming, we played badminton and table tennis and spent many fun evenings by the barbecue. The Balinese gazebo became the focal point of family gatherings.

I love to swim, which surprised a lot of people. I was pretty fast for a chubby kid. I felt this was my secret superpower. Every time I got in the pool, I would surprise everyone with my skill.

Unlike my brother, I didn't see the pool as a training ground or an exercise tool. Instead, it became my personal escape. Whenever life troubled me, and problems hounded me, I could head out to the pool, dive under its cool surface, then glide across the water, using long purposeful strokes, cutting swiftly from end to end and leaving all my cares behind. Swimming became a from of meditation for me. Back and forth I'd swim, lap after lap, letting my troubles evaporate.

When I returned to Lahore after my prolonged captivity, I found myself swimming again. Part of my motivation was that, after many years of starvation, I'd started gaining weight at an alarming rate. But part of what drew me back to the water was that sense of freedom and escape the pool had always promised.

At dusk, after the family dinner has been cleared away, with my daughter safely tucked in bed, I'll slip into my swimsuit, step outside, and hit the water. The moment I break the surface, I am weightless. My battered, scarred body can float free and slice through the water with grace and ease. It is liberating.

After my swim I listen to the birds at dusk as they gather in the towering trees around.

Often, as I sit at home, poolside, dripping and marveling at this everyday miracle, this oasis of escape, I think back to my days in captivity. In particular, those six days spent traveling to Afghanistan.

On forgotten trails, outrunning bombs.

The hardest six days of my life.

And the place I think of most of all is the mountain.

I can't tell you the name of the mountain. Yet to see this mountain on Google Maps would hardly portray its existence in my memory. The mountain was the culmination of a brutal, unforgiving landscape that nearly became my graveyard. If I'd died on that mountain, and many times I was certain that I would, my grave would be unmarked, my death unremembered, my life ended amid the most treacherous ground I'd ever encountered. I faced this fact every hour of our trip.

We were twenty-five men in total, trekking by foot. We were the last ones to leave Shawal: Muhammad Ali, the remnants of his intelligence corps, Sohail, and me. The women and children had gone on ahead via a different, more forgiving route, as they could travel safely in the open and were not in danger of being picked up or targeted by the army. The men had to travel by smugglers' routes, which meant days on dangerous trails, outrunning bombs.

Those were the worst six days of my captivity. Worse than solitary confinement, worse than being tortured, drugged on ketamine, and smuggled blindfolded in a burka covered in my own vomit. Those six days on the mountain were marked by exhaustion, and the shroud of death hovered over us at all times. The days were grueling, a trial for someone in the best of health and a misery for someone such as me.

To make it to Afghanistan, we had to travel for days by foot over mountain trails on our way to meet a truck convoy that would transport us to Gomal, the first point where we would break our journey. We had to navigate trails that hugged the sides of steep cliffs, where any misstep would send you tumbling into a seemingly bottomless chasm. We walked all day and rested at night as best we could among the jagged rocks. As we traveled, bombs fell around us. Army jets scoured the mountains. They dropped payloads of fire. We'd walk until we were bombed, then we'd scatter to hide. We were typically bombed twice a day, sometimes more. We'd be walking or running the rest of the time. It never stopped. Just bombing and running, running and bombing, until we were so exhausted we'd feel like we would fall over. You believe you can't go on. But you have to. You can't stop. You have to keep going. The bombs don't stop, so neither could I.

As we walked, Sohail and I kept each other distracted with talk about soccer. "What the hell happened since Fergie left the club?" one of us would start, and soon the other would follow. We talked at length about United player transfers and glorious moments in club history as the mountains shuddered and the world around us literally crumbled. The jet fire was constant. We didn't know if we'd survive the next moment.

"I am the mountain breaker!" I once boasted to Sohail as we crawled through the snow on a trail. "That's what you've got to call me from now on." To urge ourselves on, we set targets in the distance and walked to them, then set new targets. This was a ritual in a game of survival with only one real rule: keep moving. Over those six days, it didn't matter at all that I was the victim and these men were my tormentors. On that mountain, we were all just men trying to live, walking on foot through some of the world's most dangerous terrain with an entire army on our tail.

So we walked, ran, hid, and occasionally crawled. Many times during our trek, as Sohail and I trudged across the rocks, trailing the other men, we heard the roar of jets overhead. Then came the reliable thud of bombs as another strike shook the mountain range. Sometimes the bombs fell terrifyingly close. As we ran from the fury, my lungs would burn, and I'd feel that my heart would burst. I had not exercised in years. My muscles had withered away and they simply couldn't handle the stress.

Through it all, I was never thinking about what exactly I was moving toward. Only a single thought was in my head: *I must live.*

I was resigned that I would never make it home, that I would never ever enjoy the life I once had. But I refused to give up.

Many times on that mountain my body gave up.

Yet, I managed to keep going.

Finally, fatigued, I fell to the stones, depleted. I told Sohail, "Go on, I'm not going to make it."

He stopped a few yards ahead of me. The rest of the men trudged on, ignoring us both. "Come on!" he shouted at me. He knew that if we stayed in one spot for too long, we would not survive.

"I can't," I said, gasping for breath. "You go."

If I lay here, the bombs would eventually find me; it didn't matter. Where was I running to? More months or years in a mud hut! This mountainside was desolate and lonely, but that day it seemed as good as any place I had seen to die.

"Get up!" Sohail shouted. I knew he could see that my carrying on was not an option anymore.

To this day I can't say what combination of emotions led him to do what he did next. I'm sure he'd grown fond of me after all our many hours of conversation, but I feel he knew that he'd be severely punished by Muhammad Ali if he lost the life of the *tilla*, "the golden ticket." It's hard for me to know what value if any I held, this stranger whom they snatched from the street in a suit who now lived and ate among them; this infidel who argued religion with them; this *kafir* who taught their children how to speak a new language.

As the bombs rained down around us, Sohail pulled me to my feet and carried me on his back.

The trek continued for six days, after which we reached the top of the mountain. When Sohail and I sat down to catch our breath, I looked out over the valleys that stretched in all directions. It was peaceful, the scenery poetic. Without the bombs, without the jet strikes, what stretched out on all sides was untouched earth in the shadows of majestic mountain peaks. It struck me that these were the same vistas you might have seen if you'd sat on this mountain a thousand years earlier. Clusters of pines swayed in the wind. The silence, for a moment, was unbroken.

Behind us the entire valley was on fire. The few people who lived there were scrambling to escape, running from their burning homes to climb up over the next ridge. The remnants of corpses were scattered everywhere. I remember thinking that if there is a hell, then this is what it looks like. Fire everywhere, the dead splayed on the ground, and nothing but the sound of human misery.

We were close to the border of Afghanistan, ready to make our descent into a new country. On the mountaintop, though, among the wind and rocks and pines and silence, concepts such as borders had no meaning at all. It's long been the tradition that the tribal groups that call this region home travel freely from country to country, crisscrossing national borders, following trade routes that are nearly as old as the stones themselves.

I knew that once we completed our journey down the narrow trail, we'd find cars waiting to take us to our next destination in Afghanistan, across the border from my native country.

The wind swept through my hair. The fresh air chilled my lungs. The landscape before me felt as untouched and alien as if I'd found myself on a distant planet. Sitting on the mountaintop, a strange feeling overcame me. I knew for certain my captors could no longer hurt me. That part of my ordeal was over. Nothing they could physically do to me frightened me or could be worse than what I'd already endured. Maybe they would kill me, but if that happened, even then I knew I would be in a better place, reunited with my father. I felt strangely calm and liberated.

Yet I knew I had never been farther away from my home than I was at this moment. My wife, my mother, my family, all those friends who had stood by me and were praying for me, they may as well have lived in a distant time. On that mountain, I was as alone as I'd ever been in my life. I had no idea what the next few weeks or months held for me. Perhaps death, just as Muhammad Ali had foretold. Even if my captors did not kill me, the environment would. The mountain, the war, the unending violence, erupting all around us without warning. It seemed likely that it would claim me soon enough.

Perched on that mountain, I was certain I would never return home.

With my back to Pakistan, Afghanistan lay ahead. If I'd felt a million miles from Lahore before, now I felt as if I'd traveled to a new world. *I'll just be fighting to live until the day I die*, I thought; *there's no other way that this can end*. Every day felt like being in a boxing ring getting knocked out. You keep trying to stop from falling, but when you do, you convince yourself it's worth it to get back up. I felt a sense of triumph having made it this far, but it was absolutely impossible to conceive that I'd ever return to my old life.

But I would return, and once I was home, I'd often think of that moment on the mountain. One song always reminds me of that overwhelming feeling of hopelessness. A song by Adele.

When I got back, I heard the global hit "Hello," playing everywhere, from every car radio, in every café, with its now-familiar lyrics:

> *Hello from the other side*
> *I must've called a thousand times*
> *To tell you I'm sorry*
> *For everything that I've done.*

Even though I know the song was written by a woman in England about the heartbreak of a long-over relationship, it always speaks to me about that moment on the mountaintop. It reminds me strongly of that feeling of being stranded between two worlds. On the mountain, I believed that no matter how far I had come, I would never be able to go back. I thought of my family and how much I missed them. I thought of my brave, innocent father and what he would think if I gave up.

Somehow, against all odds, I had made it to that mountain.

Now I had to go on.

I did not know for how long, but I knew that I could not be defeated because I would never give up.

**Across the mountain vehicles waited for us. We collapsed,** exhausted, in the flat beds of the pickup trucks that carried us toward the village that would be our new home. The accommodations in Afghanistan were even more rudimentary than in Mir Ali. Arriving in Afghanistan was like traveling back in time. At Muhammad Ali's home there had been proper toilets. In rural Afghanistan, the tribes don't believe in toilets. I'm not sure they even know what toilets are. Instead, you head out into the wildernesses, find a spot, and do your business.

The first thing we did when we arrived at our new settlement was to get digging. In this way, the Uzbeks were very organized. Their makeshift new home was to accommodate two dozen people. We were living provisionally now. New rooms were built and pits were dug for human waste.

We arrived in a valley of Zabul province on January 1, 2015, and after that we would shift accommodations every few months. In Afghanistan, we were reliant on the hospitality of the Afghan Taliban. This simple fact ruled our lives. But Muhammad Ali, in all his arrogance, seemed to quickly forget this. His indifference to his hosts eventually led to a massive miscalculation, and then an outright betrayal. It also set in motion a series of events that would topple our world by the end of the year.

For six days on that mountain, I tried to imagine what Afghanistan held. What would be my fate. Probably more misery leading to a sorry end. But never in my wildest imagination did I think that this country would hold freedom for me and my eventual improbable path back home.

# 28

The negotiations for my release, now into their fourth year, felt like an absurd exercise in futility. Once we were in Afghanistan, under Muhammad Ali's supervision every few weeks Usman Majid would contact my mother and resume making impossible demands. Muhammad Ali remained convinced that my family was holding out over money and that the government would release the terrorists on his list. Each time I would accompany him to a local bazaar in Zabul, where he would call from a pay phone. Often I was speaking to my father-in-law because the strategy was to refuse me direct contact with my mother.

I would scream and tell my father-in-law this was a stupid plan that was only worsening my situation, but in return he told me he was only doing this for his daughter. Otherwise, he would have washed his hands of this entire affair long ago. I later learned that this was merely a tactic and not a reflection of his true feelings, but at the time it was hard to hear nonetheless.

In Afghanistan, there was nothing. Just two people on the phone with what seemed like a thousand miles between them having the same pointless conversation going nowhere.

Muhammad Ali's demands never wavered. There was no room for negotiation. My bloodied fingernails and a collection of horrific videos had so far not yielded the desired result. Now that the torture had stopped and we'd relocated to Afghanistan, he had less leverage than before. Had he been an astute negotiator, he'd have traded me long ago for whatever my mother was able to offer. But if I'd learned one thing about him over the years, it was that he overestimated his intelligence. He was rigid and obstinate, with an ego that ultimately cost him his life.

Often I'd stand by the pay phone as Muhammad Ali ranted at my father-in-law. Deflated, I realized my life lay in the hands of two angry men who'd locked horns. Despite everything around us falling apart, Muhammad Ali after each call ended would optimistically insist he was making headway. Which he clearly wasn't.

As for the list of men whose release he'd demanded, their names were mostly meaningless by now. Some had already been freed, some were dead. The only three names that mattered were those of the men who'd been captured from my kidnapping, since their continued confinement was the one thing keeping me alive.

Two others on that list, however, came to be very important. I'd met neither man previously. They'd been released in the last few years and had, by 2015, made their way back to Afghanistan. We were destined to cross paths. These two would now play a pivotal role in the events that nearly led to my death and, eventually, led to my release.

Neither they nor I understood that they had carried the piece to my freedom back with them to Afghanistan, like the last piece to solving the puzzle that held me in captivity.

**One man was Mullah Jannat Gul, the same Taliban leader** who, years ago, after his release, had accompanied Haji Khalil-ur-Rehman Haqqani to Miran Shah during his failed negotiation for my freedom. Jannat Gul was known to Muhammad Ali, and since that failed negotiation, Jannat Gul had returned to Afghanistan and swiftly risen through the ranks of the Taliban. By 2015, Jannat Gul was the Taliban's head of intelligence, a crucial role because of the rumored death of the Taliban commander, Mullah Omar, the infamous leader who had not been sighted since 2001. Mullah Omar had in fact died of hepatitis C, and his death remained a closely guarded secret, unknown to Taliban allies. The Taliban leadership sensed that, without their influential figurehead, their grip on the region would falter.

The second man was Mansoor Dawoudullah, the younger half brother of Mullah Dawoudullah, a senior Taliban commander who'd been killed in a raid in 2007. Mansoor Dawoudullah had been released from prison as part of the ongoing peace talks with the Taliban in 2013. Each time a high-profile prisoner such as this was released, one who'd been on Muhammad Ali's original wish list, he would react jubilantly, taking it as a sign that the opposition to his demands was crumbling, but I knew the release had nothing to do with me.

Freed, Mansoor Dawoudullah made his way back to Afghanistan and found himself in the midst of the crisis surrounding Mullah Omar's death. Another major factor was at play in the region: the rise of ISIS in Iraq and Syria. A group viewed with justified horror in the West, ISIS was at the height of its infamy in 2013 and was a source of inspiration to extremists in Afghanistan, Pakistan, and beyond. The group's flagrant and horrific stunts, its beheading videos and torture propaganda, had lent it a ferocious appeal among other self-styled jihadis. ISIS proclaimed itself a new Islamic caliphate. It welcomed all jihadis to join the fight. Despite his family ties to the Taliban, Mansoor Dawoudullah saw ISIS as the rising force in the region. He planned to renounce the Taliban and swear allegiance to ISIS and enlisted Muhammad Ali and the remains of the IMU to join him in his betrayal.

I knew all this because Muhammad Ali talked incessantly of nothing else. After so many years, he finally felt he and his mercenaries were an integral part of a great uprising. Together with Mansoor Dawoudullah they decided to convince the Taliban to join ISIS or they'd sever ties with the Taliban completely. Either way, Muhammad Ali's deranged vision of triumphantly marching into a conquered Rome seemed, to his mind, closer than ever before. I questioned the wisdom of abandoning the group offering protection, but Muhammad Ali had little interest in my opinion.

When Jannat Gul paid Muhammad Ali a visit to confer with him and Mansoor Dawoudullah, the mood was tense. The Taliban sensed they were losing control of the groups under their protection and that a strong hand was needed to unify everyone. Jannat Gul didn't mince words and issued a direct threat to Muhammad Ali. There would be no more protection either for Muhammad Ali and his men or the women and children.

Muhammad Ali and Mansoor Dawoudullah left the meeting convinced that the Taliban represented the past and ISIS represented the future, committing a grave error in not taking Jannat Gul more seriously.

**As our first month in Zabul came to an end, the children** arrived to join us. My life stabilized once again. My heart broke for these young ones robbed of their childhood, displaced and dragged to every dusty, desolate, and dangerous corner of the area.

I worked, I slept, and I taught the children. Those early days in Afghanistan had a numbing rhythm. On the mountaintop as I crossed into Afghanistan, I had said farewell to my family, resigning myself to certain death in these hopeless circumstances. Muhammad Ali had discovered Twitter, and he took great pleasure in printing out tweets from my friends and family as proof that they'd forgotten me. He came into my room one day that summer to announce that my brother Shehryar was married, showing me online photos from the wedding. He assumed I would have an emotional breakdown.

Instead, I smiled. "Good. I'm really happy for him."

Just as I was genuinely happy to find out my younger sister was married. I wished I had been able to join the festivities; however, I could only pray for their happiness and for us to be reunited. I'd long since let go of the notion that their lives would come to a standstill without me.

This was something I'd learned from my father. He'd always been the largest influence in my life, until he was violently taken away. Never once did I doubt that he'd want us to go on living. That's what I wanted for my family: to embrace life with love, joy, and togetherness, which was no longer available to me. It gave me strength to know that they were still experiencing it. Their happiness traveled across those miles and engulfed me too.

Muhammad Ali became complacent and stopped printing out each tweet. He would occasionally just show me his laptop. That was a big mistake. One day, he brought me Twitter to show me how I had been forgotten. "See? You might as well be dead," he said sarcastically. I started to wonder what the point of all this was. Why was he trying to convince me that my family had moved on? Would that make them more likely to pay? I think he just enjoyed the cruelty of it. The happiness of my family was alien to him, so he had to balance it out by evoking pain in me.

When he showed me the Twitter feeds of my friends, I spotted one tweet from my friend Umair, who had written, "Miss you bro, things just aint the same 1 love." When I saw that, my mask of bravado nearly slipped. If my friends had forgotten me, I would have forgiven them. But they hadn't; that one tweet, sent out into the world, gave me a little more strength to carry on.

I couldn't know how my brother and my sister had both agonized over whether to go ahead with their weddings. I never heard the long, tearful conversations they'd had with my mother, who encouraged them both to proceed with their plans, despite the fact I couldn't be there. My mother's philosophy throughout the ordeal was that they had to remain strong and normal so they would be able to sustain me when I returned. They were not victims, only I was. Just as I'd come to believe that their happiness should, and must, continue, my mother convinced my siblings that the best way to honor me was to move forward. I believe she learned that from my father. They all wanted me back and never gave up hope. They had much more faith that it would happen than I did. But in the meantime, they could live, and love, keeping me close in their hearts and prayers.

**As months passed in Afghanistan, far from the Pakistani** jet fighters and the ducking of their bombs, now a world away, my life seemed relatively calm. The situation between the IMU and the Taliban, however, had taken a turn for the worse. Muhammad Ali was the functional leader of the IMU, but his forces were scattered in three different parts of Afghanistan. At the insistence of Mansoor Dawoudullah, Muhammad Ali willingly agreed to pledge his allegiance to ISIS, convinced that ISIS would soon conquer Afghanistan and Pakistan. This looming betrayal didn't affect our day-to-day lives, and I assumed it would pass as just another example of the infighting that often consumes extremist groups.

It was November 8, 2015. I remember the exact date because I'd gotten my hands on the radio and was sitting with Sohail listening to Manchester United play West Bromwich Albion. Jesse Lingard had just scored the first goal of the match, putting Manchester United up 1–0. We heard the ecstatic cheering in the stadium; suddenly it was drowned out by another familiar sound: rockets.

Bombs were exploding outside our house in the Zabul valley. Sohail removed his earphone and ran outside to see what on earth was going on. I sat breathless, waiting for news, the incongruous cheers of soccer fans echoing in my ear. A few moments later, Sohail returned. He was out of breath, with a crazed expression. He looked at me with fear and panic in his eyes. All those times before, after everything we'd been through, from drone strikes to bombs pummeling us from the

sky, he had never looked even remotely fazed. He was genuinely frightened.

I had never seen that look in his eyes before.

"What is it? What's going on?"

"The Taliban have come. Prepare yourself for war."

# 29

Over the summer of 2015 I had seen the transformation in the allegiance of Muhammad Ali. He was clearly agitated by the rumored death of the Taliban commander, Mullah Omar, as well as having growing admiration for ISIS under its rapacious leader, Abu Bakr al-Baghdadi. Muhammad Ali was drawn to ISIS, seduced by their boundless violence. He praised the group's brutal, uncompromising tactics, often telling me that he thought the Taliban were weak in comparison. The Taliban had, he felt, softened, and the ruthlessness of ISIS was more to his liking.

Then in June, after years of rumors, Mullah Omar's death was officially confirmed. For Muhammad Ali this was the last straw. With the whisperings of Mansoor Dawoudullah in his ear, Muhammad Ali decided he would officially shift the allegiance of the IMU from the Taliban to ISIS. Unofficially, the group's alliance had changed much earlier. This blatant public display of defiance was intolerable to the Taliban, and it set into motion the final ghastly events.

I'm certain the Afghan Taliban did not care for the IMU, with its ragged band of a few hundred outlaws scattered across Zabul. Muhammad Ali's betrayal represented something larger: it threatened to delegitimize the Taliban. At first, his announcement sparked an ongoing negotiation between the Taliban and the Uzbeks, with threats, enticements, cajoling, and coercion. As I'd learned through bitter experience over four years, the IMU were unreliable negotiators who were not to be trusted. Muhammad Ali made a gross miscalculation, succumbing to his greed for influence and power; defying all logic, he senselessly went head-to-head into a confrontation with the Taliban.

Muhammad Ali would pay dearly for his errors. His cursed saber-rattling was to trigger a savage backlash.

On November 8, 2015, the Afghan Taliban set into motion a precise, carefully planned attack on three Uzbek camps in the Zabul valley.

The Taliban militia perched in the mountains surrounded the camps, leaving the Uzbeks with no escape. The plan was to weaken the stronghold from this vantage point by killing as many fighters as possible before entering the valley.

Outnumbering the jihadi faction, armed with superior firepower, the Taliban went into battle with a single objective: to annihilate the enemy with no intention of taking any prisoners. All the while careful to never underestimate an equally ferocious adversary.

The Taliban forces surrounding the valley from the heights had a visual advantage, enabling them to fire missiles and rockets into the camps.

In the freezing-cold dead of night, the initial burst of fire caused panic and confusion among the ill-prepared, trapped Uzbeks.

Sohail and I took cover in my room until a portion of it was destroyed by shells. Crouching in my makeshift prison, I wondered if this was the end. Had I thus far survived torture, drone strikes, and arduous treks across mountains only to now perish as collateral damage in a war I hadn't signed up for and certainly didn't believe in? We were sitting ducks awaiting certain death in a hopeless situation.

The battle lasted three days and nights, with the Taliban maintaining the upper hand.

Muhammad Ali sensed defeat. Realizing he could no longer defend the camp and capture was inevitable, he understood his only option was to initiate a dialogue with the Afghan Taliban, calling for a cease-fire.

The Afghans entertained his request, and a party of Uzbek leaders set off to sit down and start talks.

I was now forced to shift into a shelter.

Sohail and I had moved from my half-demolished cell into another room occupied by twenty-five Uzbek women and children. Sohail was tasked with guarding the women, and I was with him, disguised in a hijab. I sat impatiently agonizing over the outcome of the negotiations.

In the midst of talks, an Uzbek foot soldier sitting outside away from the negotiations got into an ugly altercation with his Taliban counterpart.

The Uzbek felt these peace talks were a betrayal to the Islamic caliphate. He leaped to his feet, drew out his serrated knife, and slit the other man's throat, killing him on the spot.

The Uzbek was then instantly shot dead.

All hell broke loose and the situation descended into chaos.

The negotiations immediately ceased, and Taliban soldiers came down to the camps from the mountain, moving quickly to butcher every Uzbek they could find. They did not discriminate between men and women; all were slaughtered.

Not knowing the outcome of the peace talks but understanding something had gone horribly wrong, in the room with me the women and children, panicked and uncertain, feared the worst.

Muhammad Ali burst into the room and announced angrily, "It is better to blow yourselves up than be taken prisoner by them!" Three of the women had been outfitted with suicide vests. Muhammad Ali's command caused shock waves. Was this to be his last instruction?

One of the women wearing a suicide vest screamed, *"Allah ho akbar!,"* and pulled the pin on her grenade.

I was petrified, then turned, pleading with Sohail to stop her. He attempted to dissuade her, but she grabbed the hand of her pregnant teenage daughter and dragged her outside, where she detonated her vest, ending both their lives.

The noise, the terror, and the debris, shook our whole world. Blood and smoke and gore were everywhere. This pregnant girl and her mother who had moments ago been standing beside us were dead, blown to pieces. Everyone in the room was screaming, shouting, or crying. Beyond that, the rattle of the gunfire from the Taliban forces echoed through the village.

I couldn't take it anymore.

Enough.

The horror of the night before, of cowering under the constant shelling, plus the infernal roar of the war outside, the bombs, the screams, the death. This was my reality. This was my life. All the pain and fear and loneliness and terror of the last four years rushed into my body and consumed me. Every moment in the last twenty-four hours, the last month, the last four years, I had wondered, *Is this when I will die? Is this the day? Is this the moment?*

I was done.

*This is where it will end*, I decided, *one way or the other*.

I stood up in the room.

Then I ran.

**In a flash, I was outside.**

I looked toward the mountainside.

A few yards away from the room where we were held was a boundary wall about four feet high. Beyond that, there was an open field. There was no time or option to think and plan. I ran as fast as possible, charging into a pack of twenty Taliban fighters. They spotted me and opened fire.

I scrambled to the ground and crouched behind the four-foot wall as the bullets ricocheted above me. The thunderous gunfire rattled in my ears as debris flew all around me.

Surely this was the end.

I could feel impending doom.

It was as though the sky were falling over my head.

I spotted an Uzbek called Bara running toward the field, unseen by the Taliban, whose attention was entirely focused on me. Initially, I thought he was trying to escape, taking the same route to the mountains I'd hoped to take. Instead he ran from behind into the Afghans, unleashing a loud *"Allah ho akbar!"* as he detonated his suicide vest. The explosion knocked me over and temporarily deafened me.

I heard Muhammad Ali's bellowing from behind, and he stuck his Kalashnikov in my face. I was unable to fathom, with the world on fire all around us, why he still cared about keeping me his prisoner. This was sheer lunacy.

I grabbed the barrel of his Kalashnikov and put it to my forehead. "End this! Finish this!"

This was it, the moment that four years had been building up to.

All the torture, the knives, the whips, the abuse, the loneliness, the running, the bombs, the scars.

The whole experience flashed before me. The gang in the street in Lahore with me passing slowly in my car; the shouts, the guns, the hood over my head, the days in a ketamine haze; the endless lonely months in Mir Ali; watching Peter the spider spin his web in the shadows of the ceiling. Every time I looked at one of Muhammad Ali's children and thought of the world of violence and pain they'd been born into and that they could never escape. That feeling I had on the mountaintop, of being suspended between two worlds, with no way forward and no way back. Knowing you've taken an unimaginable journey with no idea where it would lead, but knowing the one place it would never take you is back home.

For years, I had struggled to hold on to my hope. The hope that one day I would find my freedom.

Now that hope was gone. And for the first time, I felt free. "Do it!" I yelled at Muhammad Ali. "Set me free."

**I think my words stunned him. He wavered.**

Behind him, Sohail shouted at him to let me go. "He's of no use to us anymore," Sohail argued over the gunfire. "Everyone's dead. We have to run or we'll die too!"

I saw a moment of stillness in Muhammad Ali's eyes. I can never explain it, but in this heavyweight boxing match,

I was in my last round. I had taken every punch, and for the first time I saw my opponent defeated.

Then he threw the Kalashnikov at me. "Go. Go die!"

I couldn't tell if he thought he was giving me my freedom or pronouncing a death sentence he couldn't bring himself to carry out. I took the gun and ran back toward the field, past the charred corpses surrounding the crater. At the end of the orchard began a dense forest. Aware that the area was crawling with Taliban fighters, I fired several bursts of my gun, wasting precious bullets as no one else was around. Wading across the shallow river, I reached the mountain and started my ascent.

I climbed for seven or eight hours, giving no thought to where I was headed. For the first time in four years, I was able to make my own decisions and chart my own path. I scrabbled up the rocks toward the mountaintop. By the time I reached the summit, evening was approaching. The sky was darkening and the sounds of the battle were fading in the valley below. I began my descent to the other side, where I was spotted by a group of Taliban soldiers patrolling the mountain. They gestured to each other, shouting, and opened fire. It had begun once again.

I threw myself to the ground behind a boulder. The firing went on for what seemed like an eternity. They loaded and reloaded. I surrendered my weapon, throwing it in their direction, making them aware I was unarmed.

"*Bandi!*"—prisoner—I called out from behind the boulder. "I'm a *bandi. Bandi!*" I shouted repeatedly.

There was an eerie silence as the firing stopped. They rushed forward, encircling me, pointing their riffles. I cautiously raised my hands in surrender. They struck me with the butts of their guns, then hoisted me to my feet. Prodded along with the end of a rifle, I was marched down the mountain, across the field, past the gore-covered crater, back to the parapet wall.

Bodies of the dead Uzbeks, men and women, were strewn across the compound. Muhammad Ali, bullet riddled, was lying dead in a pool of blood.


**It's hard for me to express the feeling I had when I saw my** captor dead. It sounds strange to say, but the only comparable feeling I've ever had was on the day I saw my father's body. On that day, I had an overwhelming sense of sadness, as well as the unshakable feeling that my world had been turned upside down. My father had towered over every aspect of my life for as long as I'd been alive, so it was almost impossible to comprehend that he was gone, that he'd no longer be part of this world, part of my life, and that somehow the planet would keep on spinning without him.

With Muhammad Ali, there was no sadness, no grief, no mourning. But his death was difficult to process. It was nearly as impossible to comprehend as my father's death had been. Muhammad Ali had held my life in his hands every day for the past four years. He had ripped me away from my family. He had stolen years of my life from me. I'd been the subject of his shifting whims, his cruelty, a victim of his darkest impulses. He was the captor, I was the captive. He was the torturer, I was the victim.

Now there was only one last crucial difference between us.

I had made it. I had lived.

And he was dead.

As I was marched away by the Taliban soldiers, I knew my journey was far from over. My freedom was still in question and my survival was far from assured.

But seeing the lifeless body of that worthless man lying flat in the dust of Zabul, I felt one strain of madness had been scrubbed from the face of this earth. That justice, for one moment, had touched down in this village and my life was one small step closer to being restored.

# 30

I was led to an assembly point where there were a handful of Uzbek survivors. Nearby, women and children were in a small room refusing to surrender, threatening to detonate their suicide vests.

An Uzbek was busy negotiating with the Afghan Taliban, bargaining for their lives. Chaos ensued until finally a compromise was achieved. The women and children exited the room, joining us at the assembly point. I felt an inexplicable relief to see Aya Jaan and Muhammad Ali's family among the women and children. Herded together, we were divided into minivans and set off in a convoy. As we drove off on the narrow dirt road, I saw glimpses of Aya Jaan and the children in a vehicle in front of mine.

The journey continued slowly through a jagged mountain pass, then all of a sudden gunmen opened fire from above.

The first burst of gunfire was indiscriminate, then followed by a targeted assassination of Aya Jaan and everyone with her.

The motorcade came to a grinding halt, spewing dust. I was baffled to see a group of Taliban soldiers firing at the convoy from the mountain slopes. We were prisoners, helpless as sitting ducks. Everyone scrambled to take cover. A bullet tore through the roof of my minivan. Exiting was not an option as we were packed and huddled one over the other. It was impossible to move. We sat terrified as the firing continued.

As I peered over and looked ahead my blood went cold. The firing was focused on the car ahead that carried Aya Jaan and Muhammad Ali's family.

I cried out, distraught. They were murdering women and children right in front of us. There was no one to listen, no one to act. We could see the women in the car ahead throwing their bodies over their children. From an elevation, a rocket was fired, which dug a crater on impact. The women, hunched over the children as human shields, were all killed. I saw Aya Jaan butchered before my eyes. There was nothing we in the trailing cars could do. I later discovered this execution was carried out because the group had refused to surrender their suicide vests and grenades. We survivors were pulled out of the minivans and rounded up. The bodies of the women were dragged away to be buried.

The Taliban had accomplished what they had come to do. They'd shown everyone in the region what would happen if you betrayed them.

**A few children survived, some with severe injuries. They** were screaming, wailing, and inconsolable over their murdered mothers. I saw Fatimah pulled from the back of the minivan, her face bloodied, shrieking. She was corralled along with the other surviving children. It was the last time I saw her.

I stood in my own group of prisoners. I had been stripped from my own family, then found souls such as Aya Jaan and Abdul Aziz, who showed me some compassion and reawakened my humanity. Now they were all dead or broken. The children who'd survived were orphaned, their lives irreparably shattered. Watching them leave, I remembered Jannat Gul's threat to Muhammad Ali, that if the IMU betrayed the Taliban, they would not spare anyone, even the women and children. Jannat Gul had proved true to his word.

**We captives were herded to a makeshift prison, located in** a few shops that the Taliban had conscripted. In groups we were led before a *jirga*, a council, to be sentenced. In all likelihood we'd be executed as examples to anyone else contemplating a betrayal of the Taliban. Instinctively I disguised myself.

Yusuf Britannia: I was a British-born Christian who had converted to Islam and embraced jihad. At the sentencing, I tried to speak up, plead my case, and tell them that I was not an Uzbek.

My appeal was ignored, and I was thrown with the other men into a cramped shop that had been made into a makeshift prison. There were close to 150 men, all of whom had been captured from various rebelling factions, the IMU as well as al-Qaeda and Lashkar-e-Jhangvi, another dissident group. The room was so overcrowded, none of us had a place to sit, let alone lie down. So we slept standing up, shoulder to shoulder. It smelled terrible. We were left in there for days. A scabies infestation broke out.

After a few days, we were shoved into the back of pickups to make the long journey to a prison in Uruzgan, a province in central Afghanistan. It was winter. Eight of us rode together, shoulder to shoulder. We drove through a constant blizzard of snow. The chill blanketed us, the kind of cold that induces muscle spasms when you have no coat or adequate covering. Had I not become conditioned to the cold weather in Shawal, when Sohail and I were living in a tent, I would surely have died out there in the truck, huddled for warmth with these shivering strangers.

Three of the men in the truck spoke Urdu. "Don't fall asleep," one said to me. "You'll die if you fall asleep. You'll freeze to death." So we took turns shaking each other to stay awake.

We moved at a crawl, hearing nothing but the hum of the pickups as they labored up a trail. We watched as the eerie and unforgiving terrain passed. I'd seen nothing but valleys and mountains for the last few months; I'd never seen anything like this. The terrain was barren and lifeless. As we crossed one mountain that had been carpet-bombed, a heavy silence fell over the men. The land was scorched and torn apart, and nothing living remained. A lunar landscape, a pitiless distant planet without a blade of grass or a bird or any other sign of life.

We stopped occasionally to rest. One of these stops was at a mosque in a tiny village. As the truck pulled over, we rushed into the building to warm up, collapsing onto the straw mats inside.

Later, in the quiet of the night, I could not sleep, haunted by the muffled screams of three young Uzbek boys who were being mercilessly beaten by our guards. They mocked them for attempting to defy the Taliban. Against the backdrop of these sickening sounds and the profane abuse being hurled by the guards, the rest of us pretended to sleep to avoid attracting fury on ourselves. These beatings went on for what seemed an unbearably long time. Then we all heard a calm voice say, "Enough."

Shockingly, the guards actually stood down. More surprisingly, we realized the voice belonged to a fellow captive, a quiet young Taliban commander not older than twenty-two who was being held because he refused to fight in the war. He was called Malang, and so far he'd kept mostly to himself. But the guards respected and obeyed him. From his authoritative tone, it was clear that Malang, unlike the rest of us captives, had a special status. When we were back on the trucks, huddled together, braving the cold, I spotted Malang riding inside the cab of one of the trailing vehicles. He had a guard assigned for his personal protection. Clearly, Malang was an ally I needed to cultivate.

Finally having reached Uruzgan, we were off-loaded, blindfolded, and kicked and shoved as we stumbled up a mountain path in the night. The soldiers prodded us inside a small mud room, then locked the door. We all collapsed and passed out from exhaustion on the freezing mud floor.

The next morning, armed guards came in, pointed at me and three others, and ordered us to step outside. I immediately feared the worst: they were going to execute us under a cloudless blue sky. As I expressed my fears, one of my fellow prisoners reassured me, "They're just rounding us up for manual labor." I remained skeptical.

We trudged outside and met our head warden, a man we called Haji. He was in his midforties but, as with most Taliban, the events of his life had left him looking weather-beaten. With armed guards standing at posts on the slope above us, Haji supplied us with tools and instructions: we were to build a road to the top of the mountain. My fellow prisoner had been right. We weren't going to be killed, just put to work. I almost laughed with relief.

I was exhausted from the physical exertion and trauma of the last few days; slaving to build a road was unthinkable. Because I'd come so close to death, I'd developed a taste for defiance. Now in prison under different circumstances, knowing that no one knew me, I developed a novel strategy. Instead of obediently taking up the tools and getting to work, I started breathing heavily, feigning a wheezing sound on each inhale. I shook my head slowly from side to side.

Haji looked at me inquiringly: What was the problem?

I continued shaking my head, held up one hand, and told him I was unable to do it. He appeared amused and asked why.

"Haji, I just can't. I almost died last night as your guards kicked us up the mountain. I was unable to breathe and collapsed several times. I am really unwell. I have a serious medical condition. A hole in my heart. A condition I was born with. I could never attempt anything physically demanding."

I have to say, I spun this story well.

Haji kept looking at me. Then he asked gently, "Who beat you? Which guards?"

"It was the guards who took us to our rooms last night." I also mentioned that we had no mats or bedding to sleep on, and that we'd almost frozen to death.

Haji turned his attention to the guards and declared in a loud voice, "No guard will touch this one! And he will not be given any manual labor duties!"

Just like that, I found myself sitting on a ledge, soaking up the warm sun for the rest of the day, and concealing the biggest smile I'd had in months.

**Was I aware back then of the irony of finally being freed** from my Uzbek captors only to be thrown into a Taliban prison as a suspected Uzbek traitor? Of course, but I was shocked to still be alive. I was haunted by the horrors of that village. The slaughter, the suicide bombings, the massacre of the women and children on the mountain pass. I no longer thought in terms of sense or nonsense, probable or improbable, believable or unbelievable. Now all that mattered was to somehow survive.

**When I was a kidnap victim, my predicament had a certain** logic. I was a hostage who would either be exchanged for ransom or killed. Now, in this Afghan prison, who was I? What was my purpose? Was I Shabby T? Or Ahmed? Or Jee Bhai? Or Babuji? I knew the name Shahbaz Taseer meant nothing to anyone here, and with my long beard, uncut hair, and filthy *shalwar kameez*, I looked exactly like every other prisoner. We were a motley crew of foreigners, traitors, and criminals, people the Taliban had no use for, so they'd thrown us all together in this prison to rot.

My experience with Haji, however, taught me one thing. I was free in this prison to be whomever I wanted to be. No one would believe my real story. But that meant I could invent the story I wanted to tell.

I could be anyone. I could be no one.

So I morphed into Yusuf Britannia.

The story of the brief life of Yusuf Britannia is strange, but perhaps not stranger than my ordeal.

During my days as a student in London, I'd met many Pakistani ex-pats who, like me, were living temporarily in England and had always struck me as a particular type. While in captivity, I'd thought often of the biblical and Quranic figure of Joseph, the one made famous for his Technicolor dream coat. A prince, he was separated from his family and left for dead in a well by his siblings, but was rescued and later came to prominence in the court of the pharaoh for his ability to decipher dreams. His story resonated with me, so once I was placed in the prison in Uruzgan, inspired by the story of Joseph, I decided I too would succeed. I was determined that I would become Joseph—or, at least, a version of him, but a character of my own creation. No one believed I was Shahbaz Taseer, and I quickly understood that revealing my identity would endanger my life. Yet I was no longer bound to the Uzbeks, many of whom, including Sohail and Abdul Momin, were now imprisoned alongside me.

So I introduced the persona of Yusuf, complete with a fantastical backstory. (Britannia was the surname I gave him, though I never mentioned that to anyone else.) I'd lived in London, I told everyone, before moving to Afghanistan to become a jihadi, and I'd been swept up in this Taliban feud. The other prisoners could relate to the notion of being a holy warrior, mistakenly imprisoned; they all claimed to be similarly innocent. My tales of London added more exotic glamour to enthrall them, given most of them had never been beyond Pakistan or Afghanistan and had barely visited a city anywhere.

The Taliban prison in Uruzgan was crowded and dirty,

though not as bad as the place they'd initially held us in. Over a hundred men were confined to a large courtyard, where we'd eat and sleep and, for the most part, be left to our own devices. Many of the prisoners spoke Urdu; the ones who didn't, spoke Pashto or Uzbek. Prisoners found inventive ways to pass the days, fashioning makeshift chess pieces from stones and pieces of paper, then drawing a chessboard in the dirt. People passed time exchanging stories. Thanks to the adventures of Yusuf Britannia, I had some of the best stories of all.

I befriended a few young Pakistani men, fighters who'd wound up in Afghanistan to join the great fight but ended up on the wrong side of the Afghan Taliban. They'd seen and done terrible things in their lives, but thrown together with them in this prison, dealing with hours of endless boredom, I was reminded of all my friends back home. These were basically kids. Murderous youths no doubt, but I tried to look at the lighter side of life. The predicament of these young men struck me as a micro-version of the larger conflicts going on all around us. Most of them were petty criminals, born poor with no education and few options. They'd been swept up in conflicts they barely understood and had no control over. All of us had been washed up here, like shipwreck survivors, in this dusty prison yard. The Taliban weren't cruel to us. Mostly, we'd been warehoused, a problem to be dealt with later.

I hadn't had anything resembling a friend for quite a while. The closest I'd come was Abdul Aziz, and I had not seen him since Shawal. I had no idea where he was or whether he was alive.

There was a man we named Qari Zalzala, meaning "earthquake," as one night he had a loud wet dream in his sleep. For all of these men packed in together, there was no promise of any sort of sexual relief. With no privacy at all the occasional wet dream was not unheard of. But this guy created a ruckus. We were all sleeping close together, so it was hard for him to hide it. He woke up with a start to see all of us laughing around him.

"What happened to you?" someone asked him.

"I guess there was an earthquake in his dream!" someone else joked.

Thus he acquired the nickname Qari Zalzala.

This was the fate of these men who had signed up for holy war, but found themselves stuck in a Taliban prison. The absurdity of it was not lost on anyone. "We're imprisoned by fellow Muslims because we're so eager to kill each other," one of them lamented. "All the *kafirs* are laughing at us." My situation was likely the most bizarre of all, but Yusuf Britannia kept that closely guarded secret.

**The strangest part, at least initially, was that I now shared** a cell with the men who'd been my captors. Sohail was there, and Abdul Momin, the troll whom I despised. One day, the Taliban soldiers began rounding up the Uzbeks, who normally stuck together. They asked Abdul Momin where his allegiance laid. He claimed innocence, saying he had nothing to do with the IMU.

"That's not true," I shouted out. "He's with them."

He turned to me, fear and panic in his eyes.

"He's an Uzbek." I didn't hesitate. The words were already out of my mouth before I'd thought through the consequences. Though if I had, I don't think I'd have acted any differently.

Over Abdul Momin's loud protests, the Taliban guards dragged him away. Moments later, they shot him.

I felt no sympathy for this man who'd taunted and tortured me, who'd done all he could to treat me as less than a dog.

**Sohail, however, managed to keep his head down and** avoid the dragnet. I never spoke up against him. We kept our distance, though. For all he'd done for me, I could not look past that he'd participated in my torture and in keeping me captive all those years. Plus, in the prison he seemed defeated and lost, nothing like the brash kid I'd come to know. His father figure, Muhammad Ali, was dead. The organization he'd devoted his life to had been wiped out. Now he was just like the rest of us, just like me, a man in prison hoping to make it to the end of another day and not be found out for who he really was.

**Over the next few weeks Yusuf Britannia became quite** popular. I would lead the men in morning prayer. I lobbied the guards for better treatment and conditions; occasionally I succeeded in my requests. We convinced the guards to bring us more hot water, so we could bathe at least every few days. This was a major victory, given we were a hundred men in squalid conditions.

Most of the time our guards were just as bored as we were, so they'd often sit down and play games with us.

We brought out the makeshift chessboard, but the guard insisted we destroy it, saying chess was *haram*.

Having had this same argument about chess with Muhammad Ali, I was well prepared for the debate. "Chess builds up the mind! 'The greatest war generals in history all recommend it,'" I said, quoting my father.

The case against chess was its physical representations of

people, a practice that is *haram* according to certain interpretations of the Quran. But we had so few pleasures to pass the time in prison, and besides, we didn't even have real chess pieces. We definitely weren't about to give up our game. A few of the prisoners, the Arabs in particular, played well. Our games were the highlight of otherwise dreary, uneventful days.

Eventually, the guards conceded and agreed to look the other way.

Once again, Yusuf was victorious. I felt smug.

Malang, the soft-spoken one I remembered from our journey, the one who seemed to have some sort of clout, pulled me aside. "Don't do that again. It's dangerous." I was drawing too much attention to myself, he explained.

This was the first time I was aware that Malang had been watching me.

Then I realized something else.

If he was observing me, he might be able to help me to get out.

# 31

Thirty days into my imprisonment it continued to be unclear what the Taliban had planned for me. Whether I was executed or released, it remained a zero-sum game. My hope hung in abeyance. Every few days the door to our prison would open, and the Taliban would release one or two captives, per their homegrown judicial process.

A part of me was envious every time someone walked out that door. However, I felt that if I was granted freedom, I would immediately be captured or become a prisoner to someone else. Where would I go? How would I get home? We were still in the middle of Afghanistan in the middle of a war. As much as I wanted to leave, I was safer in prison than traveling alone in this part of the world.

My only hope, I reasoned, was to find someone with status who could assist me on the outside. Someone who could not only get me out of prison but provide safe passage back to Pakistan.

Until now, I'd believed that was an impossible goal.

Now for the first time there was a glimmer of hope.

Malang had been a respected Taliban commander; however, he'd refused to fight the Uzbeks, and for this insubordination he was being made an example of in jail. He was treated with deference by the guards and obviously had connections outside the prison. Yusuf Britannia was doing well in the prison, but it was time for Shahbaz Taseer to bring out the chessboard and make his first move.

This move wasn't without its fair share of risk, since revealing my identity might have led to a worse fate than my current situation.

If I'd miscalculated, Malang could have used my real identity as a bargaining chip for his own release.

After weighing the pros and cons, I devised a strategy, cautiously approached Malang with trepidation, and revealed my identity to him. I figured he would either see the benefits for him in helping me or he'd use this information to harm me, but either way, this was my best shot.

He seemed intrigued by my tale but skeptical. I tried to think of ways in which I could sway him. I mentioned my one Taliban connection, that a high-ranking Taliban commander had served as a negotiator on my behalf in the early days of my captivity way back in 2012. I hoped this would bolster my story and establish that my family had some kind of pull with the Taliban.

Malang listened intently as I recounted the rigors of my abduction. However, when I mentioned a Taliban commander had tried to negotiate my release, he cut me off right away. "Who was it?"

"A high-ranking official."

"A name. I need a name."

It was a reasonable request. The problem was that I had only heard the name once in passing, a few years earlier, while being tortured. So my recollection was a little hazy.

As soon as I hesitated, struggling to recall the name, Malang dismissed me impatiently. What I'd hoped would be a detail that would confirm my story had convinced him that I was bluffing. He'd seen me interacting with the Uzbek prisoners on occasion and had no reason to trust me. The sum of the parts of my story were not adding up. He needed that name, he said. Without that, he couldn't help me.

Then he walked away.

Any chance of freedom hinged on a simple detail, my ability to remember the name of a person I'd never met and whose name I'd only heard once.

**Determined not to give up, I retreated to another part of the** yard. Malang, I now believed more strongly than ever, was my ticket out of this current situation.

Over the next four days, I approached Malang repeatedly, hoping that I might find another way to convince him of my legitimacy. I promised him that my family would take care of him, that I'd pay him a sizable ransom for my release. He told me the Taliban do not believe in holding hostages for ransom. I could tell I was getting close to the point of angering him with my persistence. Every day I beseeched him, and every day he had the same reply.

He needed that name.

On the fifth day when I approached him, Malang almost smiled as I got closer, or maybe he winced. Yet I felt my stubbornness was paying off. Perhaps he'd figured that if it was all a con, I would have given up long ago.

He told me he liked me and he could see that I was not like the others in the prison. But, he said, there was still nothing he could do for me.

"Tell me, why do you keep bothering me?" he asked, almost amused.

"Because I have nothing to lose."

Then I did something crazy. I launched into a long story about my father and how he got his start in business.

I'm not sure what I was expecting to come of this. The tale was from a world that had nothing to do with the one I found myself trapped in. This kind of story seemed unlikely to impress someone like Malang. But I was not thinking all that through. I simply started talking.

I could tell Malang was listening.

And I managed to cause a chink in his armor.


**My father, I told Malang, was only twenty-four when he set** up a chartered accountancy firm called Taseer Hadi. In the early seventies he moved to Dubai to expand the footprint of his company. As he struggled to establish himself, an acquaintance mentioned to him a lucrative opportunity that required making a pitch to the rulers' right-hand man, Mehdi Tajir. Tajir was completely inaccessible and time was of the essence, but my father learned that Tajir would be returning to the United Kingdom, where he was the United Arab Emirates' ambassador, from Dubai. Thinking on his feet, my father booked seat 1B in first class, next to Tajir.

Once on the plane, my father casually approached the gentleman and said hello; they started chatting. For the next few hours, they talked about art, literature, history, culture, travel—all my father's favorite topics. I knew firsthand that

Abba was a captivating speaker on the subjects he felt passionate about. Sure enough, listening to him, Tajir could not believe he was so young. Tajir was so impressed that he agreed to award the contract to my father.

With that, my father's firm—Peat, Marwick, Taseer, Hadi—had a successful start in the Middle East.

It was a risky move. My father did not even have the money for a return ticket home from London. If he'd failed, he would have been stranded, scrambling to find a way back. But he took the chance because there was no better option and knew his future depended on it.

When I finished, Malang smiled. My story had gotten to him. "I can't help you." But this time, he added something else, something he hadn't said before: "From the inside."

I could tell I'd made some headway. I'd started to persuade him.

Still, he needed that name.


**Another day, another miracle.**

As I approached Malang, I had an epiphany.

In an instant I recalled the name.

Haji Khalil-ur-Rehman Haqqani. The man who'd negotiated for my release. The man who'd been angered when Muhammad Ali insulted him as an "ISI maulvi."

After a frustrating period of sleepless nights, cold sweats, and clammy hands and racking my brain, the relief of remembering Haji's name enabled me to breathe evenly and gave me hope once again.

When Malang heard me call out the name, he turned pale.

He whispered something to his guard in Pashto. I had no idea what he said, but I knew there was a strong connection.

---

**On February 29, 2016, about a month after I'd first revealed** my identity to Malang, he approached cautiously, taking me aside and handing me fifteen thousand Pakistani rupees. He pointed in the early-morning light toward a hamlet across the mountain approximately an hour away on foot. Five thousand rupees was put in my breast pocket, and ten thousand was to remain concealed in my side pocket.

"Released. Walk an hour away."

I'd heard the words, but I could barely comprehend what they actually meant. What was he trying to say? I couldn't believe this was happening. I reeled back and asked him a simple question: "Why?"

He wouldn't answer that question or any of my other ones. He simply gave me instructions and said goodbye. That's the last time we spoke.

Men around me began to hug and slap me on the back, cheering and congratulating me, as if I had won the lottery, which, in a sense, I had. Before I left, I spotted Sohail and other Uzbeks sitting against a wall. Sohail looked like a broken man. Prison had not treated him well. I felt compelled to say something to him, though I wasn't sure what I wanted to say. We'd been through so much together. He'd saved my life. He'd also tortured me. His simple act of sharing that radio, of connecting with me over the Manchester United games, probably preserved my sanity. In many ways, I was thankful for him. Yet he'd inflicted so much cruelty on me and I couldn't forget that.

As I approached him, he looked up. He seemed confused, though no more confused than I was.

I leaned down and grabbed his shoulders.

"I forgive you. You tormented me in the name of God. And in the name of the same God, I forgive you."

Then I straightened up and walked away.

**I will never know why Malang got me released. I thought it** was for money, the reward I'd promised to pay, but he never mentioned it or sought a way to collect it. Perhaps he felt sympathy toward me and believed I should be reunited with my family. Or he came to believe I deserved an end to my long ordeal. Maybe he simply felt he should help any man who could claim a connection to Haji Khalil-ur-Rehman Haqqani.

I couldn't know. I didn't have any answers. Only instructions.

A few moments later, I stepped out of the large gates of the Taliban prison where I'd been kept wondering whether fate was playing a cruel trick and would I be shot in the back.

The date was February 29, 2016. That it was a leap year was significant, though not to me. I didn't know it then, standing on the doorstep of the prison, but on that very same day in Rawalpindi, a city in Punjab province, Mumtaz Qadri, my father's killer, was being hanged for his crime. The sentence was carried out in a leap year so the anniversary of his death couldn't be celebrated every year.

I walked free for the first time in nearly five years; my father's killer was being brought to justice at the same time.

I didn't know it then.

I was standing outside the door of the prison in perfect disbelief.

No joy. No elation. Just a sense of disbelief.

For the first time in four and a half years, I was free.

A barrage of questions entered my mind. I was faced with

a conundrum. Am I to exercise restraint or make a hasty escape into the unknown?

As I walked away across the mountain on that cold February morning, I was determined to leave all my bitterness behind, recalling a quote by Nelson Mandela. As I walked out the door toward the gate that would lead to my freedom, I knew if I didn't leave my bitterness and hatred behind, I'd still be in prison.

# 32

Technically I was free, but I was also somewhere in Afghanistan, amid a savage war.

I told myself two things as I walked down the mountain toward the rendezvous point where I'd been instructed to go. One: Do not be optimistic. Do not let yourself feel hope. The best-case scenario, I thought, was that Malang was sending me off with some of his men to a safer house, and after that he would start his own negotiations with my family. I envisaged that these negotiations would take no less than six months. I could not allow myself to indulge in any impractical fantasy that I was on my way to freedom. I'd been let down by false hope one too many times.

Two: I told myself that if I did find my way to freedom, I would leave all of this behind. The prison, the torture, the years of my life stripped away, the massacre in the village, the memories of seeing the children I had developed a fondness for murdered in front of my eyes. I could not take all of that with me. If I did, it would be as if I had never escaped at all.

My thoughts as I left that prison in Afghanistan were not as clear as Mandela's, and I could not dare to compare my situation to his. As I embarked on this next unexpected stage of my journey, I made a similar decision. I'd already told Sohail and the Uzbeks that I forgave them, and I had. I'd seen my captor, Muhammad Ali, dead in the dirt. I knew he could never torment me again. After all the pain, despair, and loneliness I'd endured, I would do my best to leave it behind. With each step I took in an unknown direction, I felt I was moving one more step away from the past four and a half years. Beyond that, I was uncertain of what the future held.

This was the first time in years I was truly alone. I walked for a few hours down the mountainside. The journey was tough. I set targets for myself to keep moving, just as Sohail and I had done when we'd left Shawal and traveled over the mountains. Malang had said the trek would be about an hour, but Afghans who'd spent their lives on rocky mountain landscapes like this one could move over them with greater agility and ease than me.

Finally, just as I started to wonder if I'd been tricked or confused about my instructions, I spotted something rising in the distance. I approached a cluster of primitive houses, and a group of men loitered outside one of them, by parked motorcycles. They stood idly as if they'd been waiting all day for me to show up. These men were Taliban mujahideen, returning home to Quetta. I was to be part of their cargo, just another item they'd carry on their journey.

As instructed, I handed over five thousand of the Pakistani rupees Malang had given me. He'd told me to say as little as possible when I met these men. I did as I was told. The men pocketed the money and evaluated me. They could have taken my money, then killed me, I thought, and no one would ever have known. If they'd left my body in the mountains, I would never have been found. My family had had no contact with me in almost a year and were completely unaware of my whereabouts. Even the other prisoners in Uruzgan knew me as Yusuf. I was a ghost now, a man so far from his home and so removed from his identity that I could easily disappear into the dust. This had been my situation ever since I'd arrived in Afghanistan. I was constantly facing the prospect that my story would end as an anonymous death in a faraway country, a forgotten life in a forgotten land.

Instead, the men nodded and gestured for me to get on the back of one of their motorcycles.

We set off. Was I on the equivalent of seat 1B?

**There were ten of us in all, riding on five motorcycles. We** traveled in a convoy for seven days, riding through freezing, inclement weather over unpaved paths, stopping only at night to rest. I barely spoke to my companions. They neither spoke Urdu nor English, and I could barely speak their version of Pashto. I could tell they had no idea of or interest in discovering my identity. I was simply a paying passenger, a package to be delivered. My transport had been arranged through a Taliban back channel, and these men had their orders, which was to take me along. If nothing else, they were good at following instructions.

At night we camped. By day we traveled through deserts and over mountains. Every so often we came upon these tiny hamlets that dot the mountainous landscape of Afghanistan, where mujahideen would always find willing and hospitable hosts. The people in these villages were obliged to accommodate us. They revered the mujahideen. In one town, we pulled over and a local merchant approached our group. "Mujahideen? Taliban? You need a place to stay? You need food?" he asked insistently. He invited us into his shop. There was delicious home-cooked food, something I had not seen in years. I tried to control my gluttony. My mouth was literally watering. I greedily set upon the food and ate until I was sated. After thanking the merchant, we continued on our journey.

In another town, a run-down small barbershop had a shower in the back. We stopped to clean up. Another night we slept in the back of a restaurant. This was the nature of our trip. I didn't say much to anyone for days. Malang had told me there was no need. Also I felt exhausted. The past few months were catching up with me. The battle in the village, the prison, the effort to win Malang over, my first taste of freedom. It was almost too much. I wasn't sure where I'd end up next, but I was happy to stay silent and keep moving.

One afternoon on the motorcycles, on a long stretch of desolate road, we rode into a hailstorm. Golf-ball-size hailstones pounded us. We continued on until the bike I was riding stopped. The driver pulled over and got off to inspect the engine.

The two of us stood there, in the middle of a vast lifeless landscape, staring at the motorcycle. We must have looked like two characters from a bleak comedy. I marveled again at where my life had taken me. Finally, with the help of the others, the driver got the motorcycle running again.

We headed back on the road.

A week into our journey, we spent the night at a Taliban check post, and I sensed we were close to the Pakistan border.

Immediately after the morning prayer, we resumed our journey. The greater distance between the prison and myself made me eternally grateful for Malang's intervention.

Exhausted, I sat on the back of a motorcycle, road weary from a week of constant travel over rough paths. I wondered if I would ever see a city, let alone the vibrant life I'd known in Lahore. It seemed like nothing but endless road behind us and ahead, with only the rumble of the motorcycles as a soundtrack to accompany our trip.

Then, an hour or so into our ride, I heard it. The sound of our tires on the road had changed. I knew what this sound meant, but my brain could barely process it.

We'd gone from a dirt road to a paved one, the kind that is sometimes used in rural areas but not in Afghanistan.

In Pakistan.

I couldn't believe it. This paved road meant we'd crossed the border.

For the first time in over a year, I was back in Pakistan.

I was closer to home than I'd been in years.

We'd finally arrived in Balochistan province, on the western edge of Pakistan, riding eastward toward the city of Quetta.

One more complication awaited me. As we got closer to the outskirts of Quetta, the men pulled their motorcycles over. One of them asked me if I had a refugee card. I'd need the card to get past the next check post and continue into the city. I didn't have one. We mutually decided they would carry on without me as they couldn't afford to run into any trouble at the check post, thus ending our journey together. These muja-hideen I'd spent a week with sped off, leaving me on the side of the road several kilometers outside town. I didn't even know their names.

As I watched the motorcycles recede into the distance, I realized I was finally free. A luxury I had not experienced since being taken hostage.

I fell to my knees, kissed the ground, lay on my back, and looked up at the heavens, and thanked the Almighty for this act of mercy. Alone in this vast expanse I shouted my name out loud.

"We are almost home, Shahbaz." Lying there, inspired by freedom, I challenged myself to conquer the last leg of this ordeal to make it home. This would not be easy, for I had to navigate the dangers of being captured again and had not been allowed to make judgment calls for so long.

It was not to going end here. I was still hundreds of kilometers from home, in the same territory where I'd been held captive for four and a half years. I was no safer here than I would have been if I'd run out the front door of Muhammad Ali's house in Mir Ali. It became clear I had no one to rely on but myself to return to my family.

I took my first step to my ultimate liberation.

It was a chilly day. I was delirious and overwhelmed, and I had another vision. I saw my father walking ahead, just as I'd seen him many times during my captivity. But this time, he was not holding me or walking beside me. He was walking on purposefully. Then he turned to look at me as if to say, "My work is done," as though he knew he could leave me on this road and I'd find my way home. Thinking about him on that road, I wept. I promised him I would complete this journey home safely.

My family had no idea where I was and hadn't heard from me or received any news in months. They had no idea about Muhammad Ali's clash with the Taliban or that I'd been thrown into a prison.

Much later my mother told me a story about a dear and close friend of hers, Susan Rashid, who called her frantically after saying her morning prayers. Susan said she had had the strangest encounter with my father. He'd asked her to convey a message to my mother: his job was done, he was exhausted and was now finally leaving. My mother, having no idea of my whereabouts or what was happening to me, only knew that my father's killer had been hanged and so assumed that the incidents were related. Susan Rashid is a credible clairvoyant.

I walked for a few kilometers on the empty road before I saw the first rickshaw approaching. Rickshaws are common vehicles in Pakistan and look like colorful beetles trundling down the street, a sputtering motorbike under a protective shell. I tried to wave this one down, but he didn't stop. Understandably he wasn't interested in picking up a filthy-looking man with a scraggly beard walking alongside a desolate road in the early morning.

I continued for another hour until a second rickshaw approached. I waved frantically. He too didn't stop. Finally, a third vehicle came and I stood in the middle of the road, waving a handful of rupees. He would either pick me up, run me over, or rob me, but at least I had his attention. He pulled over. I asked him to take me to Quetta. I gave him two thousand rupees from the money Malang had given me for the ride, which was a king's ransom for his services. He happily pocketed my cash, started the rickshaw, and we sped away.

As with many small outposts in Balochistan, Kuchlak is organized around a bustling central bazaar. It had no checkpoint, so I did not need a refugee card. We arrived close to midday, and the market was full of activity. Shoppers and merchants were haggling over wares, and shady mujahideen hung around at the fringes. For me, all this activity was both good and bad news. Good because I would attract less attention in the bazaar, but bad because it meant more potential dangers were lurking. With each step closer to freedom I became more and more aware that I could be snatched up again at any time, or worse.

With my unkempt appearance and dressed like a mujahideen, I blended in. My objectives in Kuchlak were clear: find a phone and avoid getting kidnapped or killed.

I spotted a small hotel and restaurant just off the main square. The large sign in front of the modest two-story building across the street from the market beckoned WELCOME TO SALEEM HOTEL KUCHLAK. Cautiously entering the establishment, I was greeted by the restaurant's owner. Ordering food, I asked if I could borrow his mobile phone, claiming I had lost mine on my trip. He refused, explaining the Taliban always managed to land him in trouble.

On hearing our conversation a young man offered the use of his phone. I dialed my mother's number.

It was March 8, 2016, a Tuesday. She didn't recognize the number coming through. My mother had been advised against answering calls from unknown numbers and had not received any calls from my captors for over six months. She was hesitant to answer an unknown number. It could have been the kidnappers.

Her phone rang again. She ignored it.

Then it rang again. Then a fourth time.

Fearing for her other two children, she finally picked up the phone.

She heard my voice instead.

"Mama, it's Shahbaz," I said in Urdu. "Do not speak to me in English." I was having trouble holding myself together, alone in the tiny restaurant in Kuchlak. I knew if she spoke to me in English, I would respond to her in English as well, which would only attract attention in the restaurant and, potentially, put me in jeopardy.

She said nothing in response. She just listened.

"Mama, I've escaped. You have to come get me. I'm in Kuchlak in a restaurant called Saleem Hotel."

My mother could barely speak. At first, she wasn't sure if she should believe this. Was it some kind of ploy? Were my kidnappers using me to draw her to Balochistan? Was this some kind of a trap? They'd tried similar tactics with her before. It seemed impossible to comprehend that I had actually escaped, that I was calling her as a free man, asking her to bring me home.

In the restaurant, I was outwardly calm but inwardly panicked. Even my quiet conversation might draw the notice of someone who'd realize who I was. Towns such as Kuchlak are breeding grounds for criminals, the kind of men who'd kidnapped me. Because my appearance was that of a Taliban myself, the young man had been willing to help me. But plenty of other Taliban swirling in and out of the restaurant might be moved to question me, hassle me, or worse. My words might fall on the wrong ears or draw the attention of some violent opportunist. I'd come too far and was too close to home to have it all ripped away from me now.

My mother had run out into the street in front of the salon where she was so she wouldn't be overheard. "Shahbaz," she said calmly, "I will get help immediately."

Hearing my mother's voice, speaking my name, I was close to tears.

"It's true, Mama. Now, please, come get me. As quickly as you can."

I knew this would be the trickiest part of all. My mother could move right away to arrange my transport, but given how far Kuchlak is from Lahore and how remote it is, it might take days to get me safely back, days during which I'd have to lie low and worry about being picked up again. It felt maddening to be so close to home yet still feel that I was stranded a world away. It would take a miracle to get me out of Kuchlak quickly.

I didn't know it, but my mother had just such a miracle awaiting me.

She promised she'd get me out and told me to sit tight. She would call me back after arranging the details.

"Please, hurry," I told her with an urgency in my voice as I didn't want to hang up. I didn't want to let her go.

"I will, Shahbaz."

The call ended.

I sat in the restaurant and ate my food, waiting forever for the phone to ring again.

When I'd first been abducted, a senior army officer, General Aftab, a thorough professional, had worked on my case. He'd always been a great support to my family, expressing personal concern and empathy.

That had been years ago, and General Aftab had long since been reassigned from Lahore to Balochistan. For him it was an important post, but my mother recalled how distraught she was when she got the news, since it meant he could no longer help on my case.

He'd been reassigned to an army base in the city of Quetta, which was about half an hour from Kuchlak, where I was sitting, waiting to be rescued.

What had seemed like a setback at the time now struck my mother as a godsend.

She reached the general and told him she'd finally heard word from me and that I was waiting in a restaurant in Kuchlak. The general told her he would find me and bring me home safely.

My mother then called my immediate family, informing them of the situation, sharing the few facts she was aware of. She told my *khala* (aunt), brother, sister, and wife not to call her as she was coordinating my rescue operation and said she was heading home to be with them.

I was getting increasingly nervous, sitting alone in that restaurant. The contours of my freedom were now coming into focus, which only made me more aware of how easily it could all disappear.

My mother called to explain a rescue team was on its way and would be there in about fifty minutes.

"What should I do while I'm waiting?"

She told me to eat some food.

She also suggested I go hide in the toilet, but I told her I'd already been there. Heading back to the loo would probably draw more attention than I'd like.

She calmly told me to stay safe and take a walk. She would see me soon.

For the second time that day, I had to cut off a call with my mother.

I waited.

It is no exaggeration to say that those fifty minutes, waiting in that restaurant, felt longer to me than the previous four and a half years in captivity.

An elite team of commandos had been dispatched, and the cavalry arrived as my mother had said. Army vehicles pulled up in front of the restaurant.

I was anxiously pacing outside the Saleem Hotel.

I spotted a number of military vehicles approaching. A team jumped out and ordered everyone to get down.

I tried to tell the soldier I was the person they had come for, but he yelled, "Stay down."

I was confused and terrified by all this. My heart raced with the thought that someone would detonate a grenade or an explosive vest and end everything.

Then I said my name out loud, which immediately got their attention.

The soldiers stepped back, saluted me, and said, "Sir, we are here to take you home," and escorted me into a waiting vehicle.

I was handed a phone, and a general introduced himself and asked me a question:

"What wood are you made of?"

"Sir, I am not made of a wood that burns easily."

"Welcome home, son."

# 33

**A**s I sat in the safety of the car, I took a deep breath, and a mixture of relief and disbelief flooded over me. Was this possible? Was I really headed home?

I'd walked into that restaurant as Yusuf Britannia, dirty, road weary, dazed, and alone, but I was leaving as Shahbaz Taseer. I could finally feel part of myself flowing back into my body. It is a strange and wonderful feeling to get reacquainted with oneself. An energy that had not been in my soul was coming back.

I could feel myself breathing again.

The army base was a fifty-minute drive from Kuchlak. When we arrived, I was taken to a room where I'd spend the night. I was to fly back to my family in the morning.

A hot shower, clean clothes, and a delicious meal of my favorite food reaffirmed that humanity still existed.

I went online to catch up with the world. I felt alive to be reconnected after being lost to the world for four and a half years. I was spoiled for choice, the whole world reopening its doors to me. Before long, two army officers entered my room to debrief me. They pulled up chairs and asked me to recount as many details as I could recall.

They inquired how I'd reached Kuchlak.

They listened to each of my answers in complete disbelief.

They had two objectives: first, to determine if after spending four and a half years among extremists I had any intelligence to share with them. Second, to find out if in those four and a half years among extremists, I'd become one. Finally they left me alone.

I had uncontrollable urges to hear my mother's reassuring voice as I sat alone in the room in Quetta, impatiently waiting to get back to life in Lahore.

I spoke to my mother, wife, sister, and brother multiple times that night. We cried, we laughed, and we talked and talked until I was spent and lay down in my bed. That's when the realization sunk in.

I had made it.

I'd survived.

I'd won.

And I was going home.

The next day I boarded an army airplane for the flight to Lahore, where I was to be reunited with my family. My heart pounded as we took off and the plane soared. Sitting by the window, I watched the miles of terrain glide by below, as though my whole four-and-a-half-year journey were happening in reverse, except now, instead of riding drugged and beaten in the back of a car, I was high above it all and the passing miles were bringing me closer to my home.

I thought about everything I'd been through. I repeated the same words to myself over and over, in my head: *My past is not my present. My past is not my present.* Everything that had happened to me till then was now nothing more than a memory. From the moment I'd left the Taliban prison, I'd set incremental goals for myself. Reach that distant rock. Climb to the next plateau. Locate the house. Meet the men. One more step, one more day, one more mile, all with the knowledge that each step, each day, each mile, was leading me back to my life.

Now on the aircraft, I set my final goal: to embrace my waiting family.

**My elated family gathered at the airport, watching the sky.** My mother, sister, brother, uncle, and wife, unable to contain themselves, created a very emotional welcome as I got off the plane and entered the private lounge. I smiled and waved as they cheered.

The moment was surreal. It felt like a dream. My mother came rushing toward me and took me in her arms, sobbing. Shehryar and Shehrbano wrapped me in hugs, as did my maternal uncle and my wife. I held them all close, overwhelmed, repeatedly thanking God this was real.

My grandmother, close friends, family, and all our staff gathered at the house to greet me. As soon as I walked in the door, the love and warmth swallowed me whole. They descended, crying, laughing, and reaching out to touch me and see if I was real.

The next few weeks went by in a haze. Everyone wanted to hear the details of my story, how I'd escaped, how I made it back. They bombarded me with questions; I answered every single one of them. I realized how hungry I was for human companionship, for the genuine love of my closest family and friends. You can't know how important it is to talk to loved ones, how crucial to your mental well-being, until you're denied that privilege for four and a half years. It had been so long since I'd enjoyed having conversations that I was soon running off at the mouth like a madman to anyone who'd listen.

I was no longer alone.

For me, what was most amazing was seeing firsthand just how strong my family had been. For all those years, Muhammad Ali had taunted me with stories about them forgetting or betraying me: my wife straying, my brother and sister celebrating without me, my mother refusing to pay my ransom. At times I'd been a fool and let those doubts take root. I saw now how incredibly more than a match they were for that ignorant terrorist and his band of mercenaries. They had hate and guns. We had love and each other. They were dead and I was home. Victory was mine.

I thought of a time, early on in my captivity, when Muhammad Ali had spoken to my mother for the first time on the phone and how overjoyed he'd been afterward. "As soon as they put the woman forward," he said to me after the call, "that's when we know we've won."

But he had never encountered a woman like my mother. She lost her husband and her son in the same year and kept going and stayed strong. She never stopped believing even when the army called her and told her I was dead. She said, "Show me the body." She said she would bring me home. Her unfaltering resolve had kept me alive, I knew it, and now here I was, home again, living proof that she was right.

I remembered the time when she faced down Muhammad Ali and told him that if he killed me, there would be no mercy, body for body, blood for blood. After one particularly tense phone call, he'd hung up after talking to my mother and said to me, "No woman is that strong. Your mother must be an ISI agent!" He was sure she'd been trained as an intelligence officer.

"No," I'd told him. "She's just a mother."

Now, against all odds, that mother was holding me in her arms once again.

**Shehryar and Shehrbano both showed me photos from** their weddings. They looked so happy, and the celebrations looked wonderful. Shehrbano told me with tears in her eyes that she'd considered hiding the photos before I returned out of shame that they'd felt so much joy while I'd been in captivity. They'd been thinking of me every day, she said.

I smiled and hugged her. "I'm so happy for you. Knowing that you were all able to live your lives, feel joy, love, and happiness, that is what kept me going. It healed me and helped me make it through."

Once home, I set about trying to reintegrate to normal life. It was strange. First there was the food. I went from stale bread to a personal chef. In no time I gained sixty pounds.

I visited the doctors to make sure I hadn't carried any ailments back with me. I still had scars on my back and on my lips where my mouth had been sewn shut and an ugly one where Muhammad Ali had shot me through the leg. When I told my physician about the various ailments I'd had, he surmised my muscles were dehydrated. Despite exhaustion, malnutrition, and multiple bouts of malaria, I suffered no permanent lingering physical effects from my captivity.

I found that I wanted to talk all the time, to tell everyone everything, yet I also felt compelled to be alone. It was a lot. To be back in my home, seeing my wife, my family, my friends, all these people I thought I would never meet again. I had become used to one small room, with no visitors, just guards coming to torment me. Being surrounded by love was an adjustment, but a welcome one.

When I needed a break, I went out to the pool. I stripped down to my bathing trunks, just me and my scars. I dove into the water, felt it rushing around me. I reclaimed that feeling I'd always treasured, of pulling through the water with determined strokes, one, two, one, two, just letting my cares trail behind me, buoyed by the water, floating free.

This story is not about what I lost, it's about what I learned and what I found. I found friendship in the most unlikely places on earth. I found love and redemption in the eyes of an innocent child. I found myself on a mountain, suspended between two worlds, unable to go back and not knowing what lay ahead. I found faith in God and strength in my family. I found my father by my side when I needed him the most, and I found out what kind of wood I was made of, and like my father, I did not burn easily.

# Epilogue

A decade on, as I reflect on my journey from being held captive by barbaric terrorists to where I stand today, I find all that was important to me, things I believed I had lost a long time ago: family, love, friendships, work, and most importantly peace. I promised myself that I would leave any residue of anger and resentment behind so I would not remain a prisoner battling my demons. Thanks largely to my father's indomitable spirit and guidance, my mother's grace, and God's mercy, I found the fortitude to overcome the fateful odds and take charge of my life.

# Acknowledgments

I dedicate this in loving memory of my abba, Salmaan Taseer, the bravest and kindest soul I ever had the privilege of knowing, and to my miracle, Serena Amy Taseer. You are the greatest gift Allah has given me. I hope one day when you read this you will understand that all my trials and tribulations led me to you and for that I wear my scars proudly.

This has been an emotional roller coaster. So much in my life has changed, but the one constant is my brave, resilient, and beautiful mother. She has over her entire life refused to give up on her children, and it is that faith that protected me and gave me the strength to find my way back home.

To my family: my aunt Tammy; my uncle Ehsan; my brother, Shehryar; my sister, Shehrbano; and their spouses, Rema and Amin. Having all of you in my life makes the sun shine a little brighter.

To my friends: I kept you with me and our memories together made me smile in the darkest of times; having the power to smile in those times is something I will be grateful for forever.

To Manchester United: you were my light when all seemed lost. You found me when I was alone, broken, and close to giving up. The sounds of the Stretford End gave my soul the strength to believe that if you could find me, then one day I would find my way back home. Glory, glory, Man United, as the reds go marching on.

To my darling wife, Neha: I'm so grateful that through this song of life I can dance with you and our son, Shavez, and daughter, Serena, as if it were an endless midsummer's dream.

A special mention to Amal Khan, Ammar Farooqi, and Adam Sternbergh for helping me throughout this book. They say the best friends help you tell your stories, and I couldn't have asked for better friends. And again to my *mamoo* Ehsan: you have protected and guided me like an older brother and best friend. Without you I would never have been able to compile my story, and for this I am forever in your debt.

Thank you to my agent, David McCormick; my wonderful editor at Farrar, Straus and Giroux, Sean McDonald; and the amazing team that helped put this together. Thank you for believing in me and God bless you all.